Achieving Guitar Artistry

Concert Solos

by William Bay

MEL BAY ®

Exclusive Sales Agent: Mel Bay Publications, Inc.
www.melbay.com

Preface

This is a collection of 56 solos which reflect a wide array of colors, textures and moods. These were originally written for plectrum or flatpick guitar but may certainly be played by the classical or fingerstyle guitarist. I have always wondered why more plectrum guitarists did not frequent the concert stage. Perhaps it was due to the lack of suitable concert solo material. I sincerely hope this collection helps to fill that void.

The solos range in difficulty from intermediate to fairly advanced. Many of them encourage the soloist to creatively utilize tone, expression and phrasing. Others in this collection are up-tempo and utilize Latin, jazz, bluegrass and Celtic rhythms. I have included an ample amount of fingering and string markings on each solo.

This is the third book in the Mel Bay *Achieving Guitar Artistry* series. It follows *Linear Guitar Etudes* and *Triads*. The goal of this series is to present material able to develop the serious guitar student into a very accomplished player. I hope you enjoy these compositions and find them to be fun to play and very enjoyable to the audience.

William Bay

Remembrance

William Bay

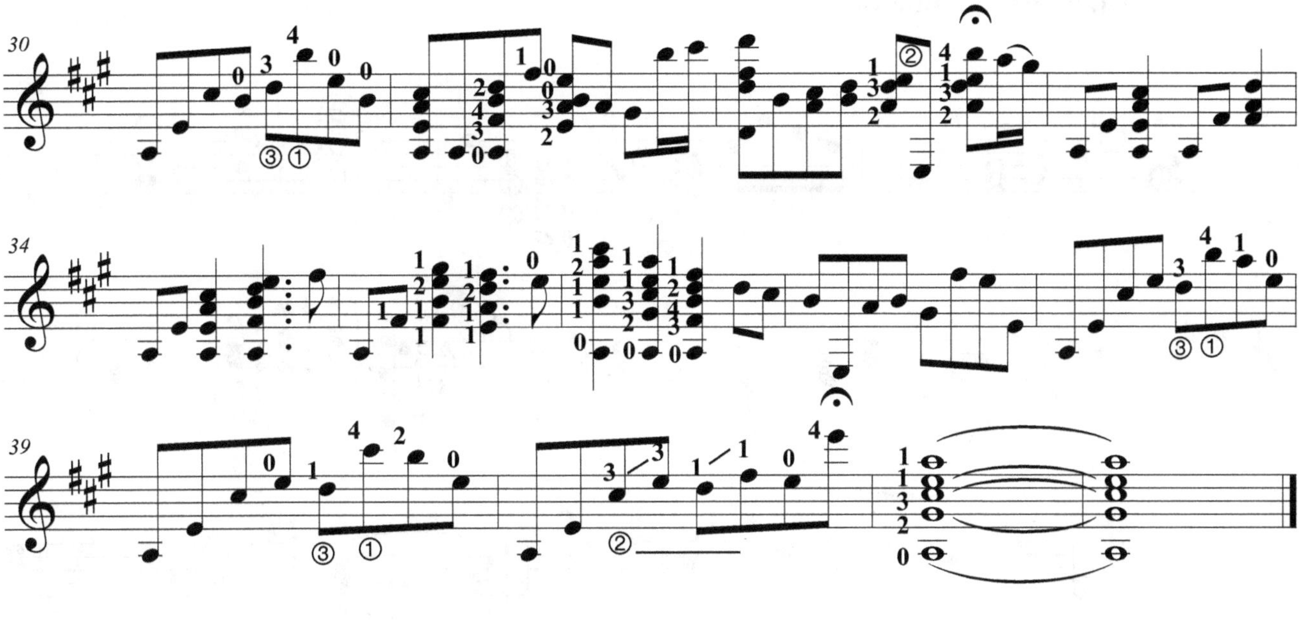
30
34
39

New Day

Andante Cantabile ♩ = 80

William Bay

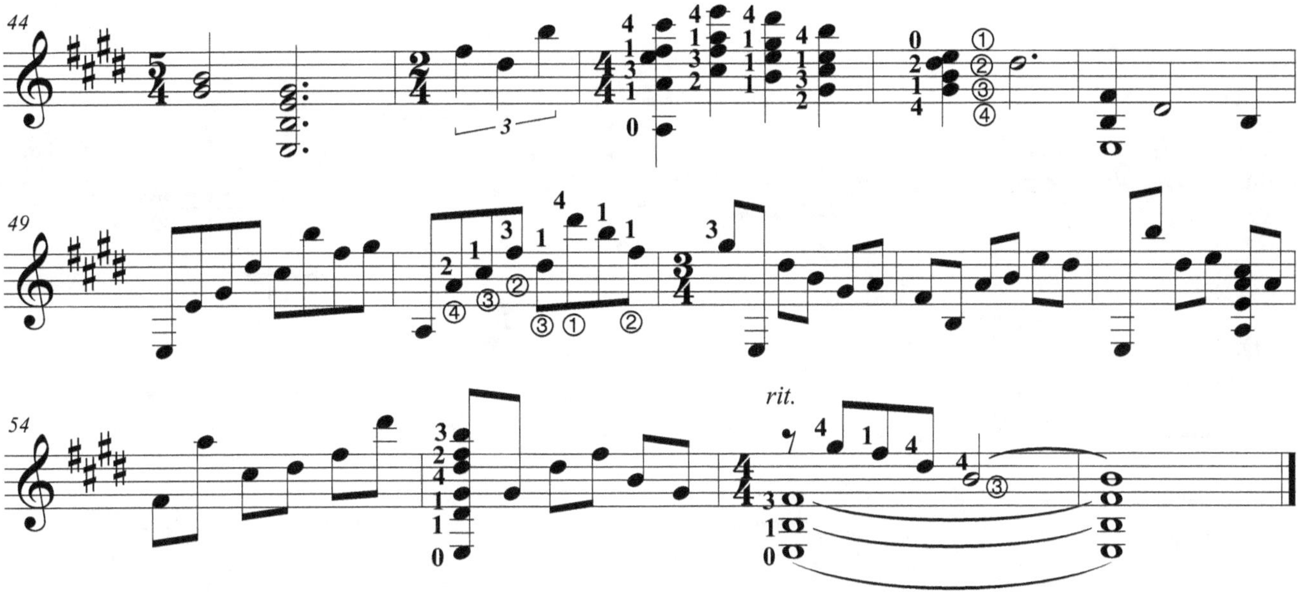
rit.

Evening Prayer

William Bay

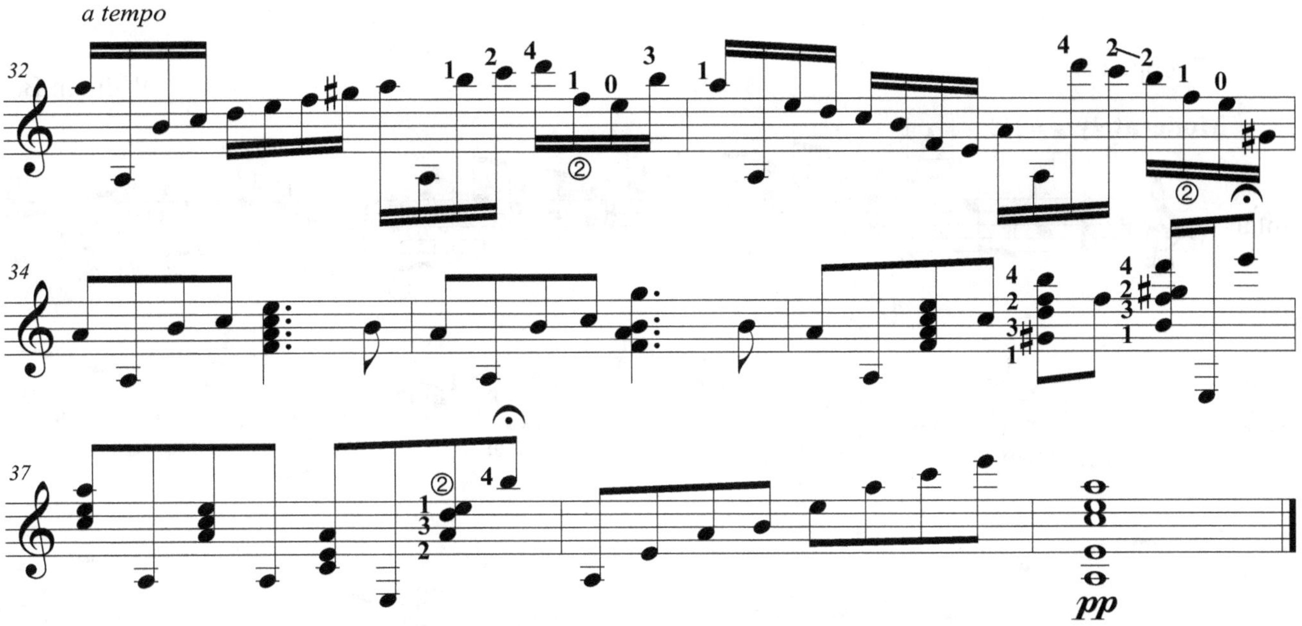
a tempo
pp

Valse and Variations

Dropped D Tuning

William Bay

Moderately ♩ = 118

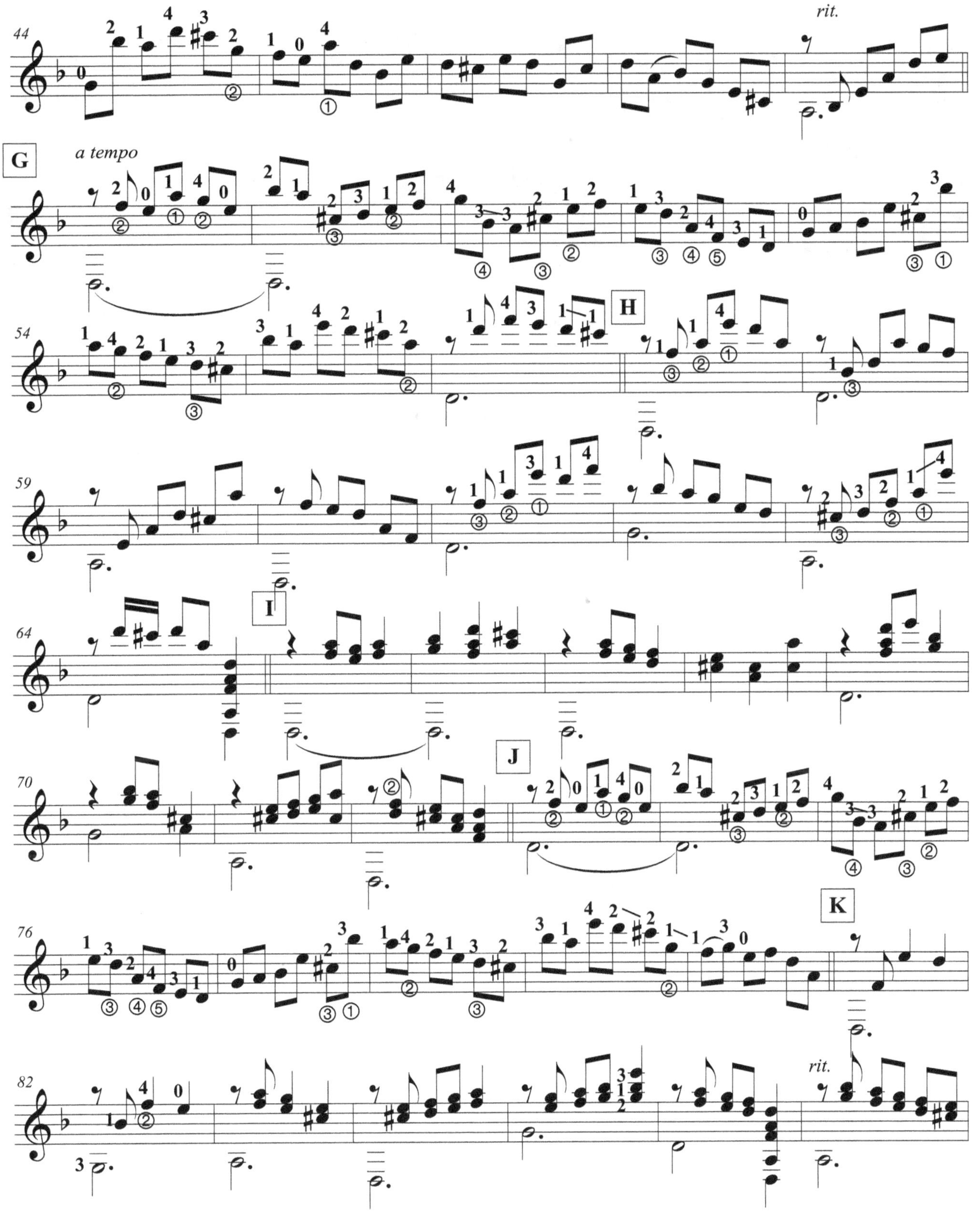
rit.
G
a tempo
H
I
J
K
rit.

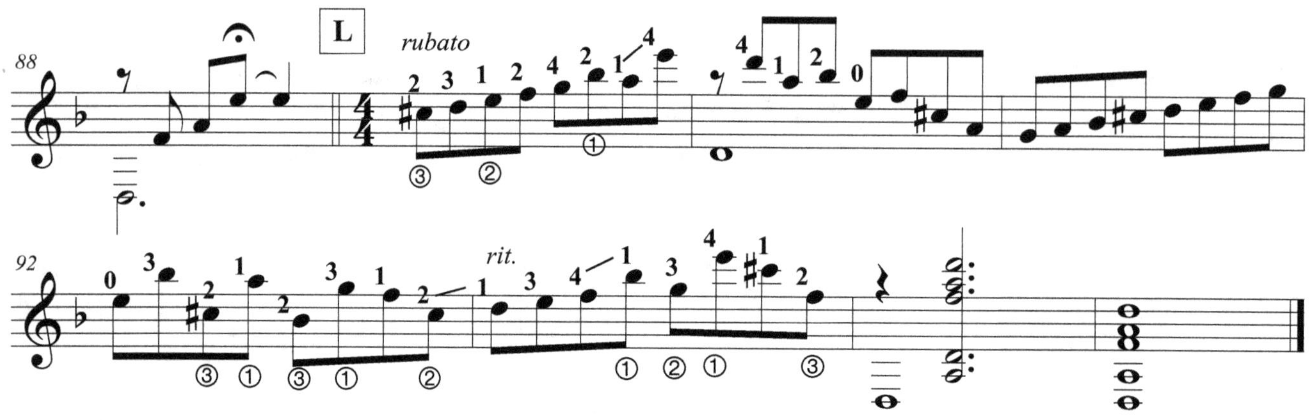
88
L
rubato
92
rit.

Canticle #1

Tenderly ♩ = 76

William Bay

Lucia

Tango

Dropped-D Tuning

William Bay

15

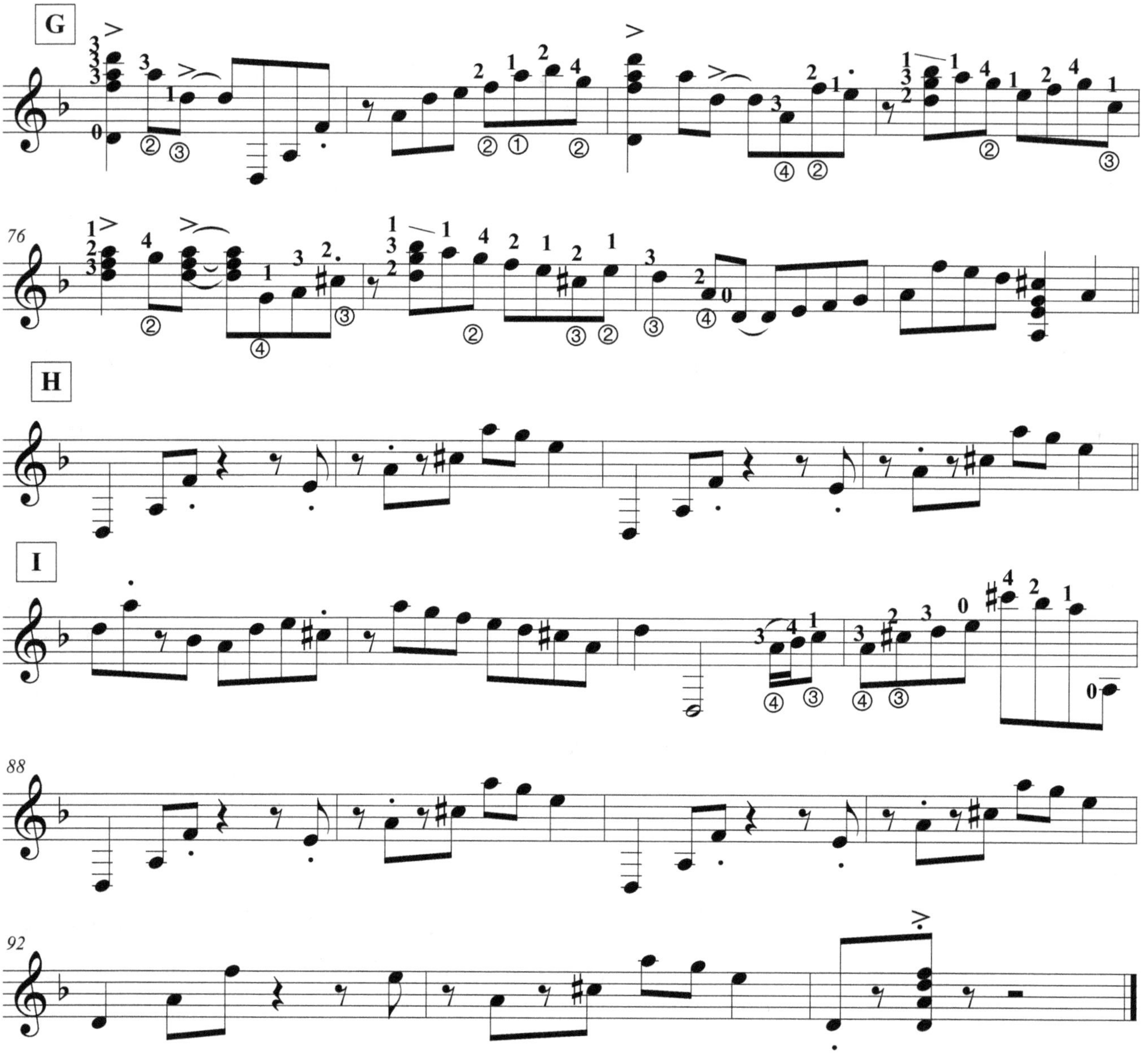
G
76
H
I
88
92

The Journey

William Bay

Slowly, With Feeling ♩ = 64

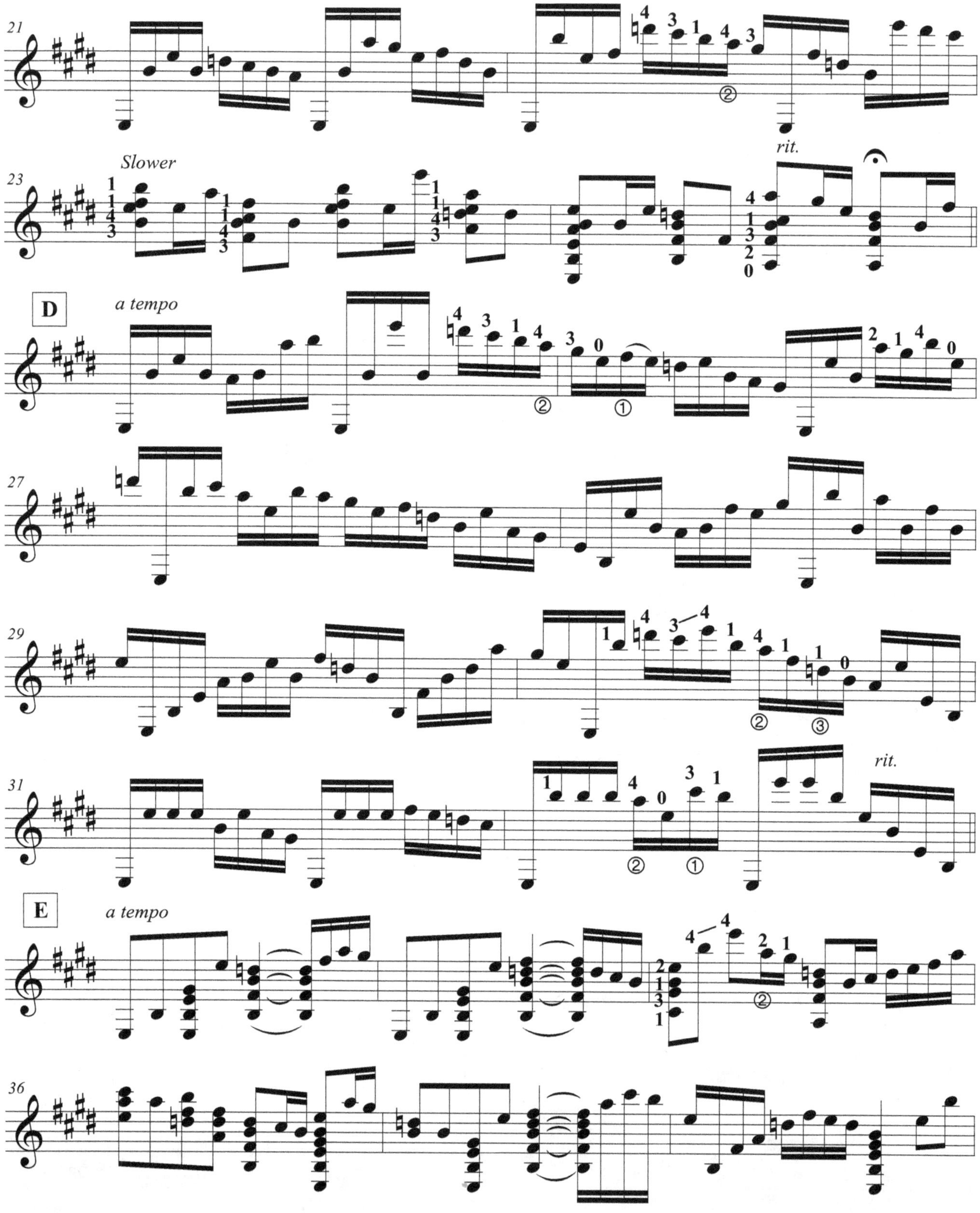
Slower
rit.
D
a tempo
rit.
E
a tempo

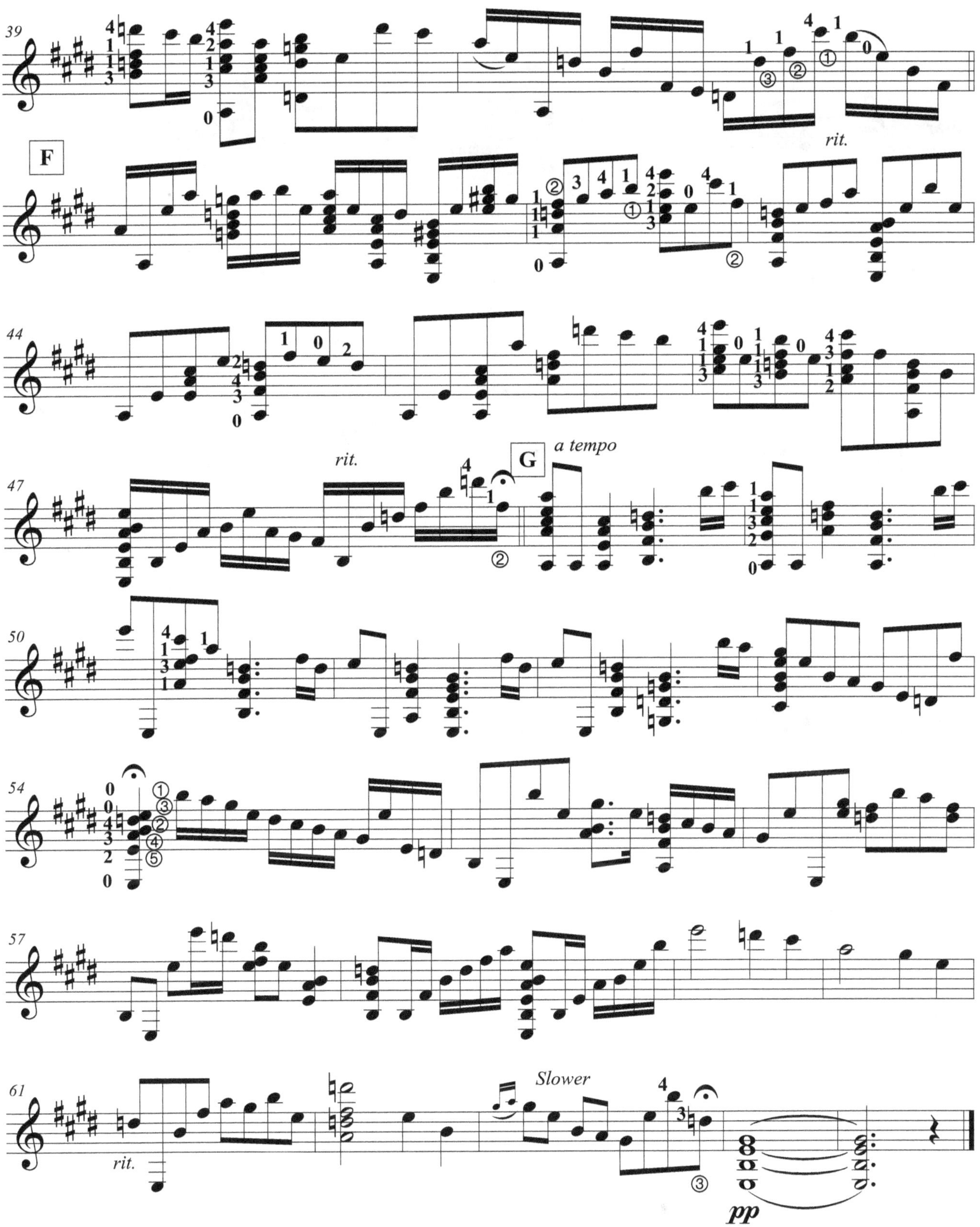
39
rit.
F
44
47
rit.
G
a tempo
50
54
57
61
rit.
Slower
pp

Dowland's Ghost

William Bay

20

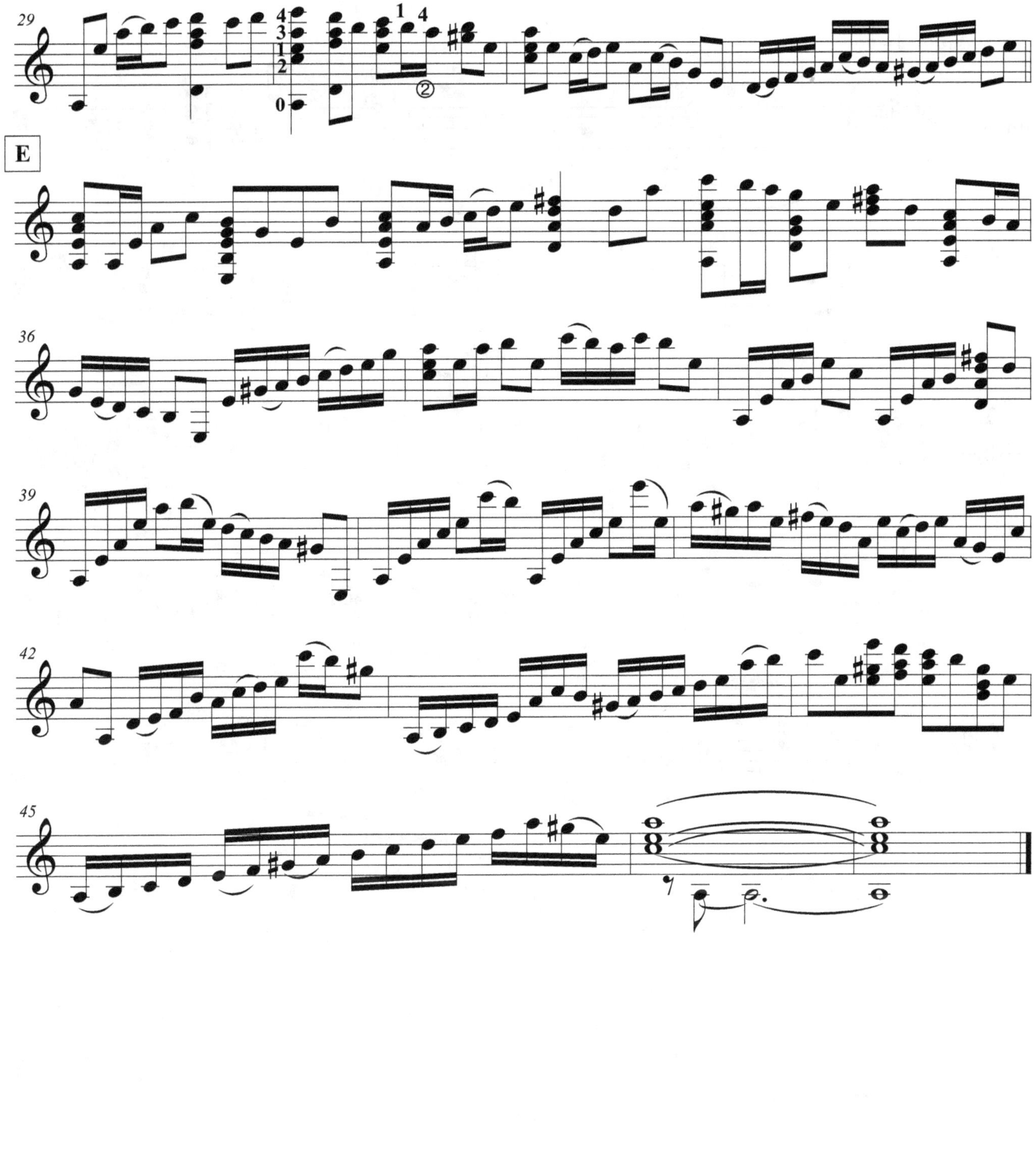
29
E
36
39
42
45

Peace

Dropped-D Tuning

William Bay

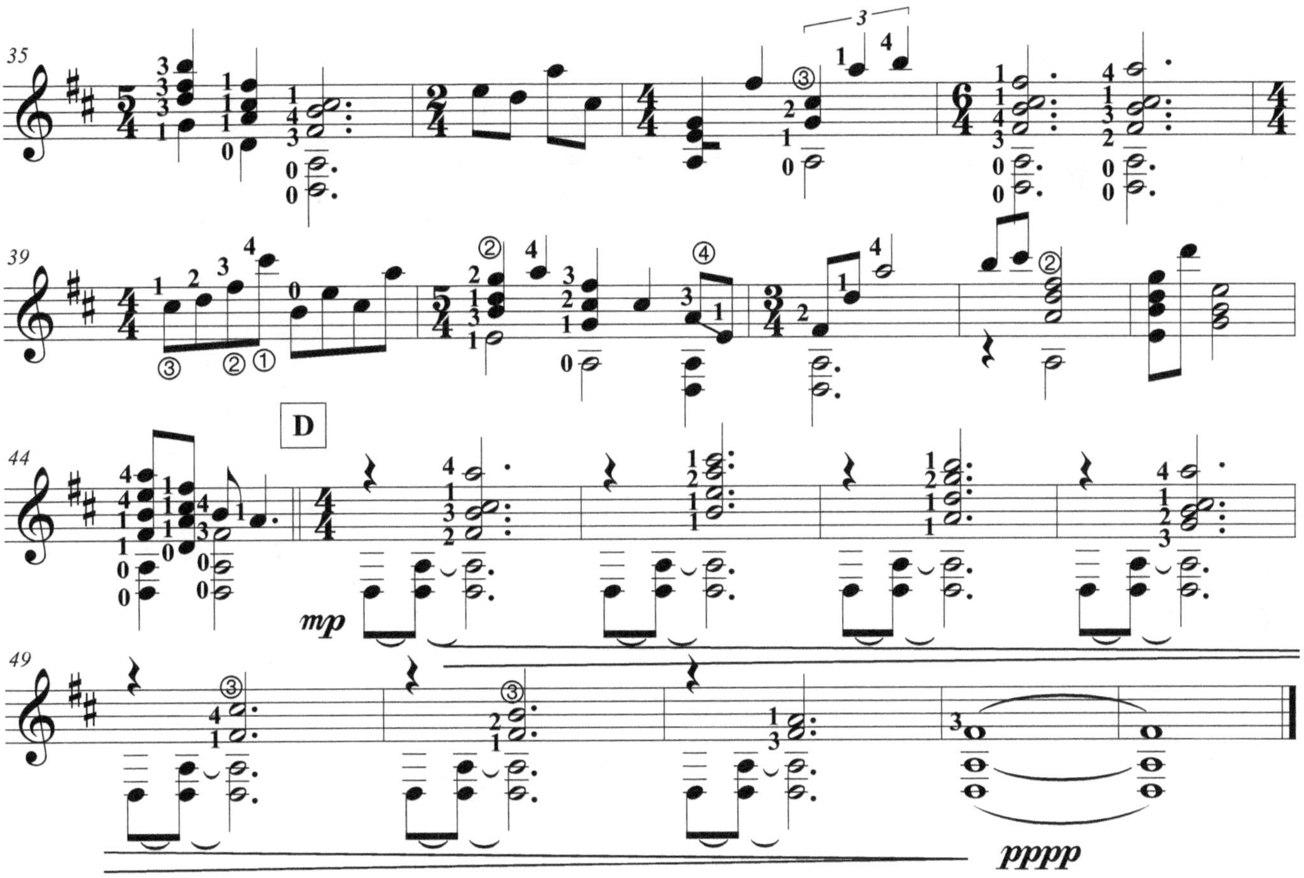
35
39
44
D
mp
49
pppp

Northern Lights

William Bay

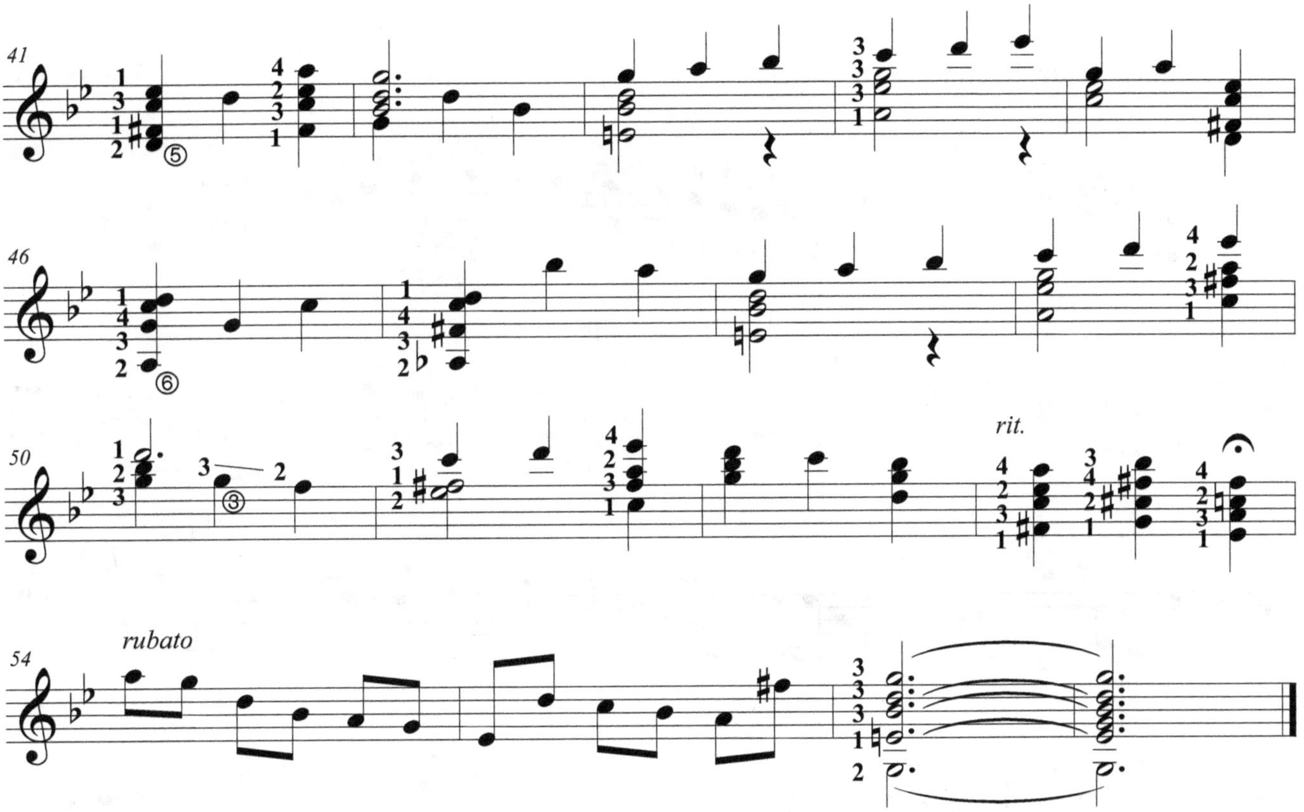
rit.
rubato

Harvest Morning

Jig

Bright, Lively Tempo ♩. = 118

William Bay

Guitar

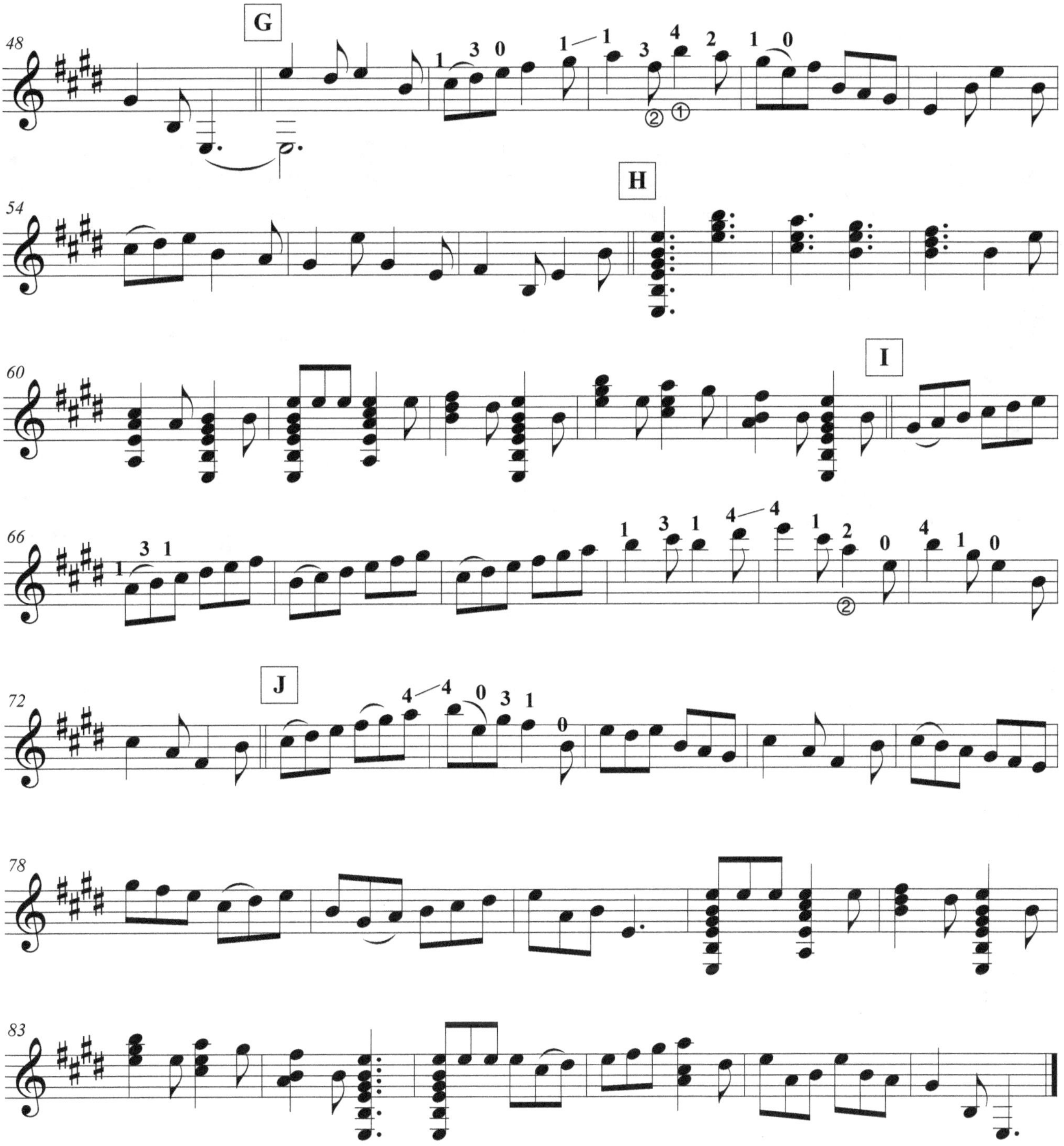
G
H
I
J

Rainfall

Gently ♩ = 100

William Bay

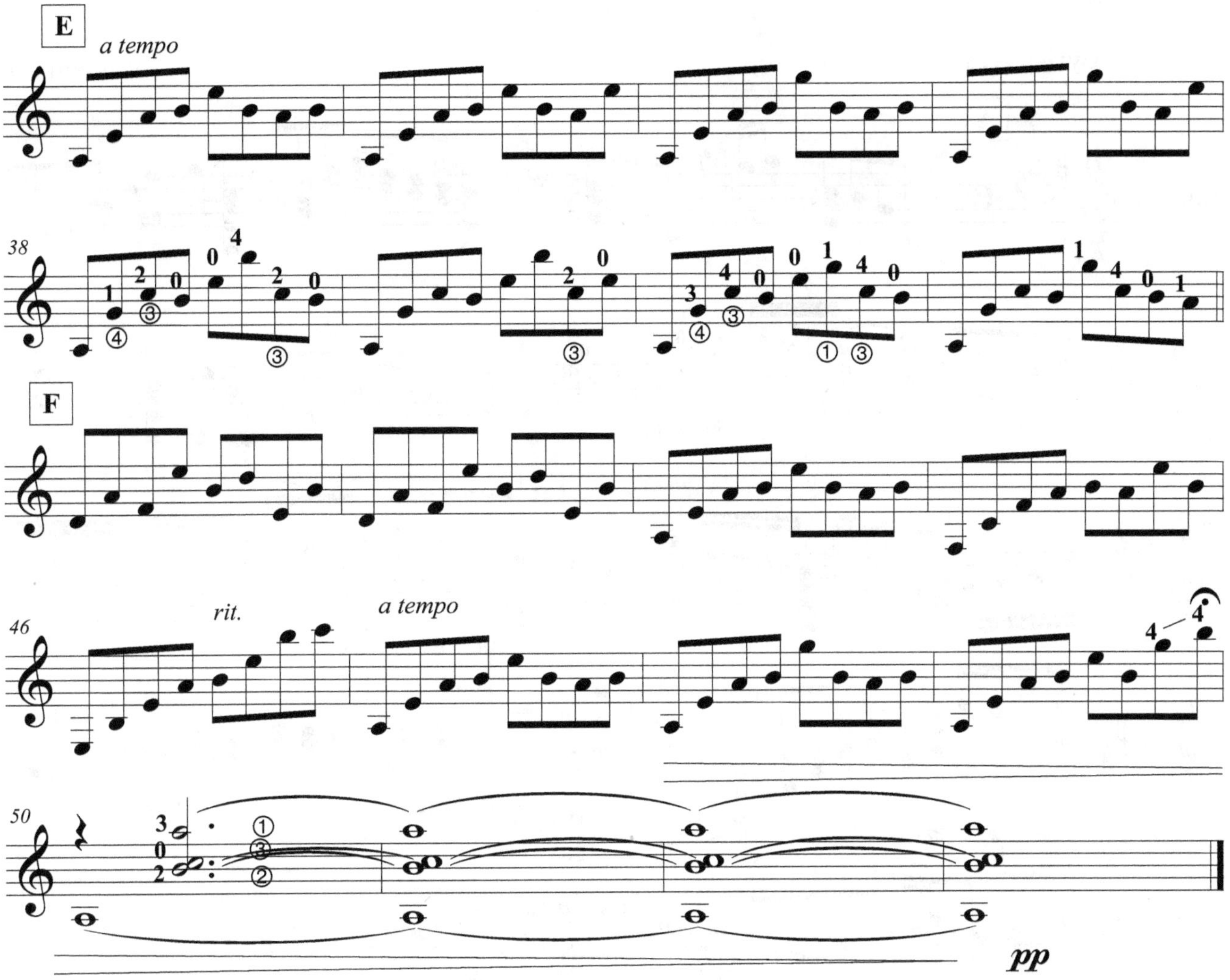
E
a tempo
38
F
46
rit.
a tempo
50
pp

Coming Home

Lyrically, Freely ♩ = 64

William Bay

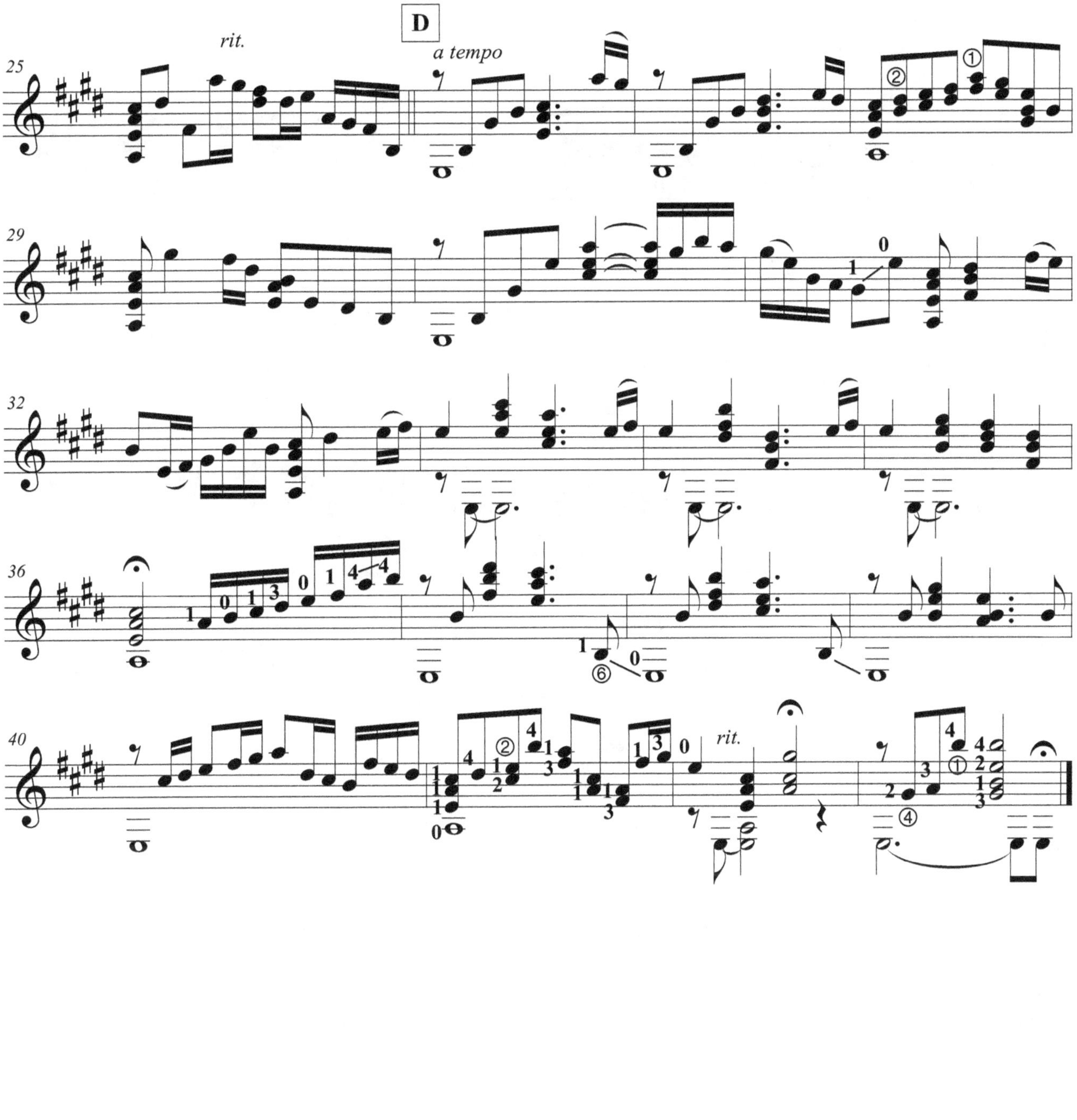
rit.
D
a tempo
rit.

Scherzo
From Sonata #1

Dropped-D Tuning

William Bay

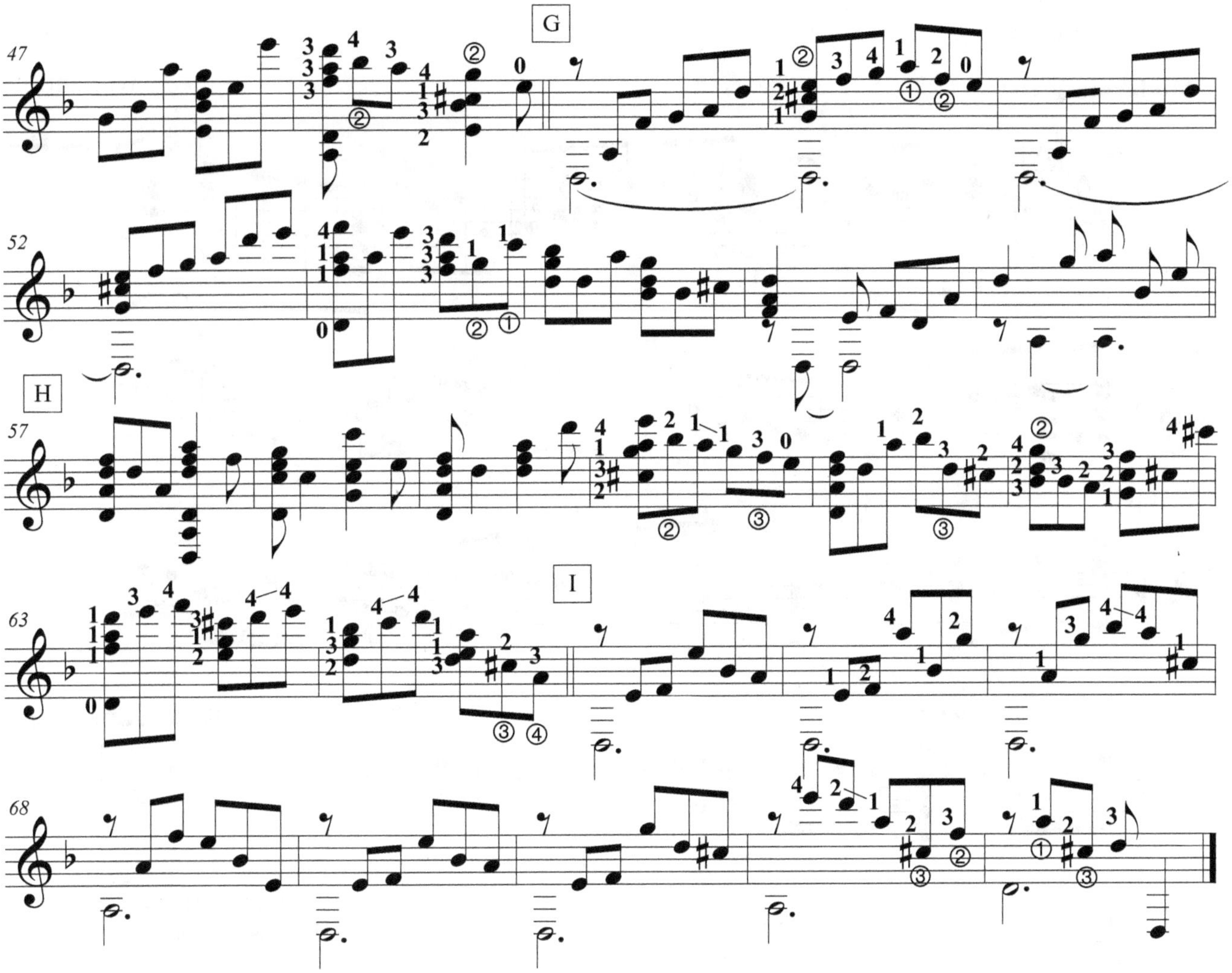
47
G
52
H
57
63
I
68

Moderato
From Sonata #1

Dropped-D Tuning

Moderato ♩ = 94

William Bay

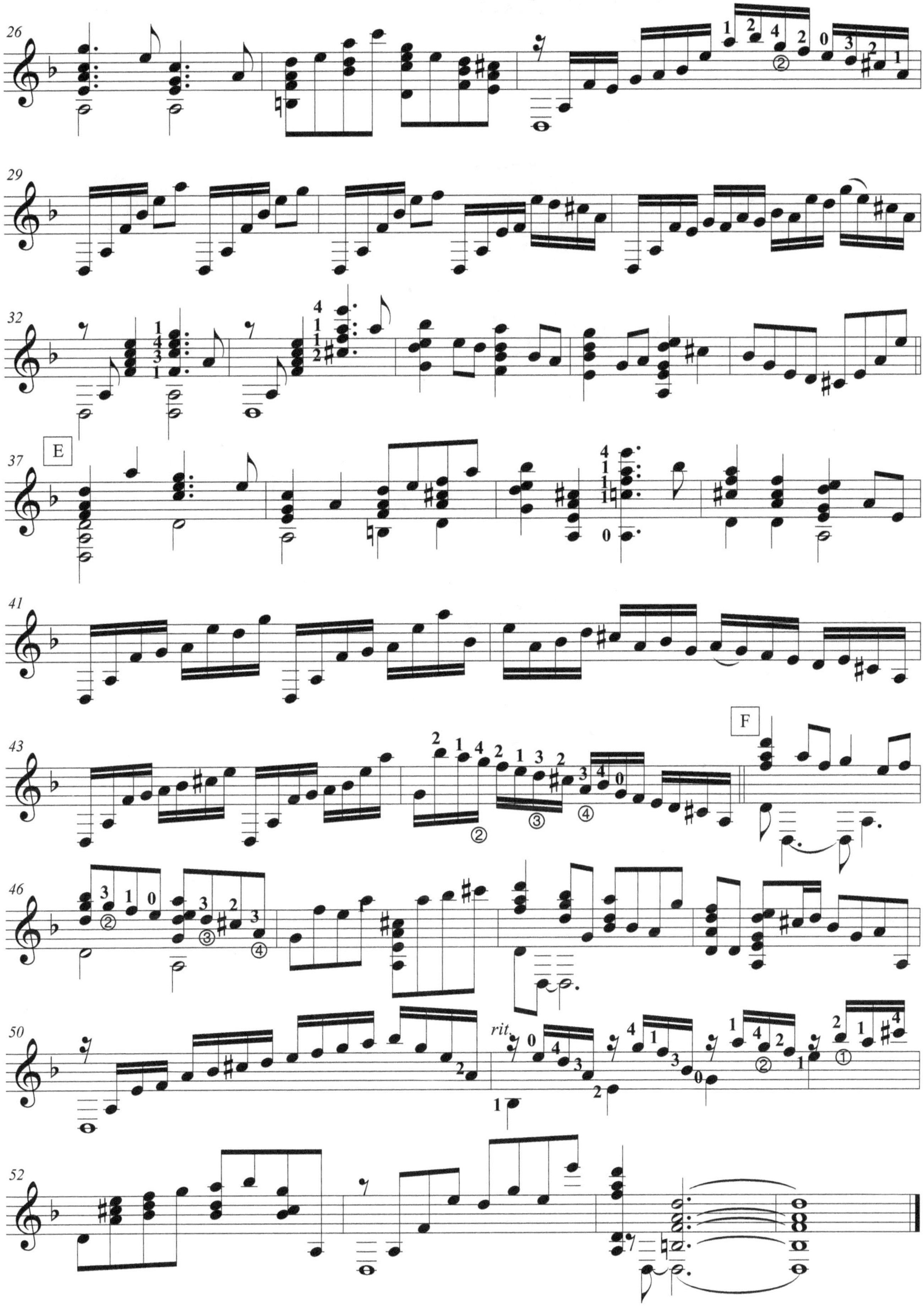
E
F
rit.

In the Quiet of the Night

Slowly, with feeling ♩ = 68

William Bay

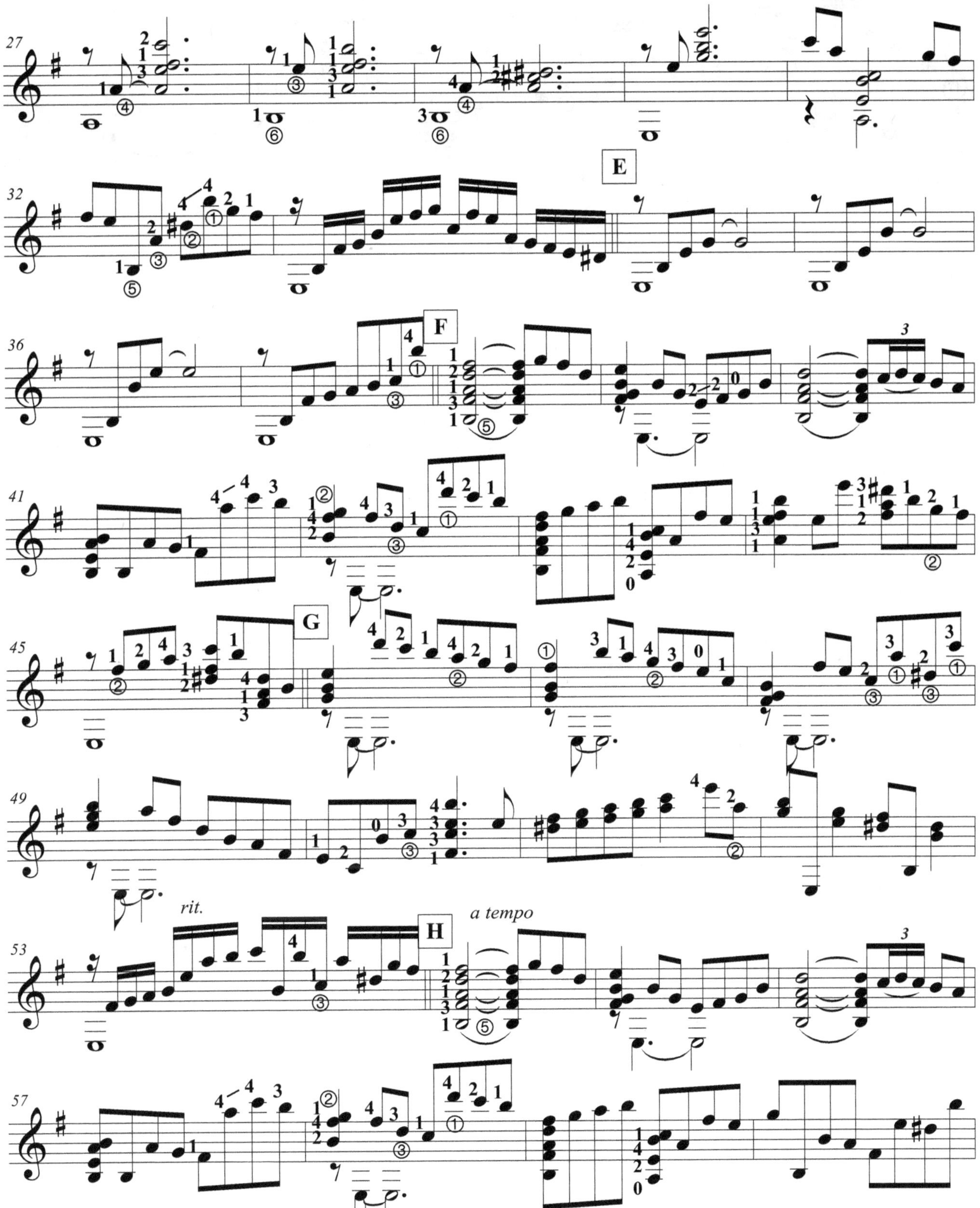
E
F
G
rit.
a tempo
H

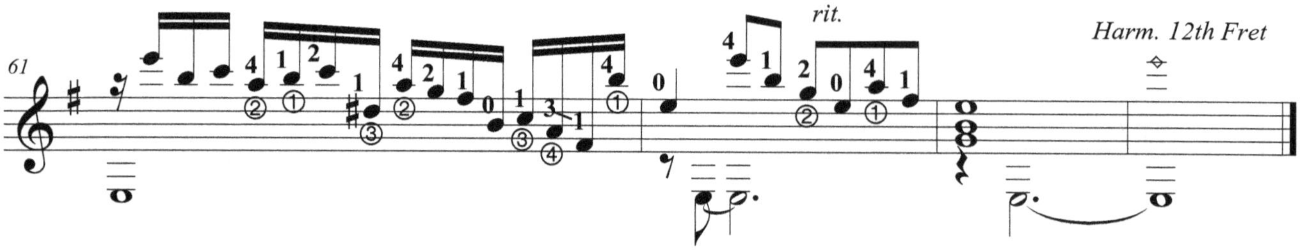
61
rit.
Harm. 12th Fret

Distant Homeland

William Bay

Fields of Culloden

Dropped-D Tuning

William Bay

Lento ♩ = 84

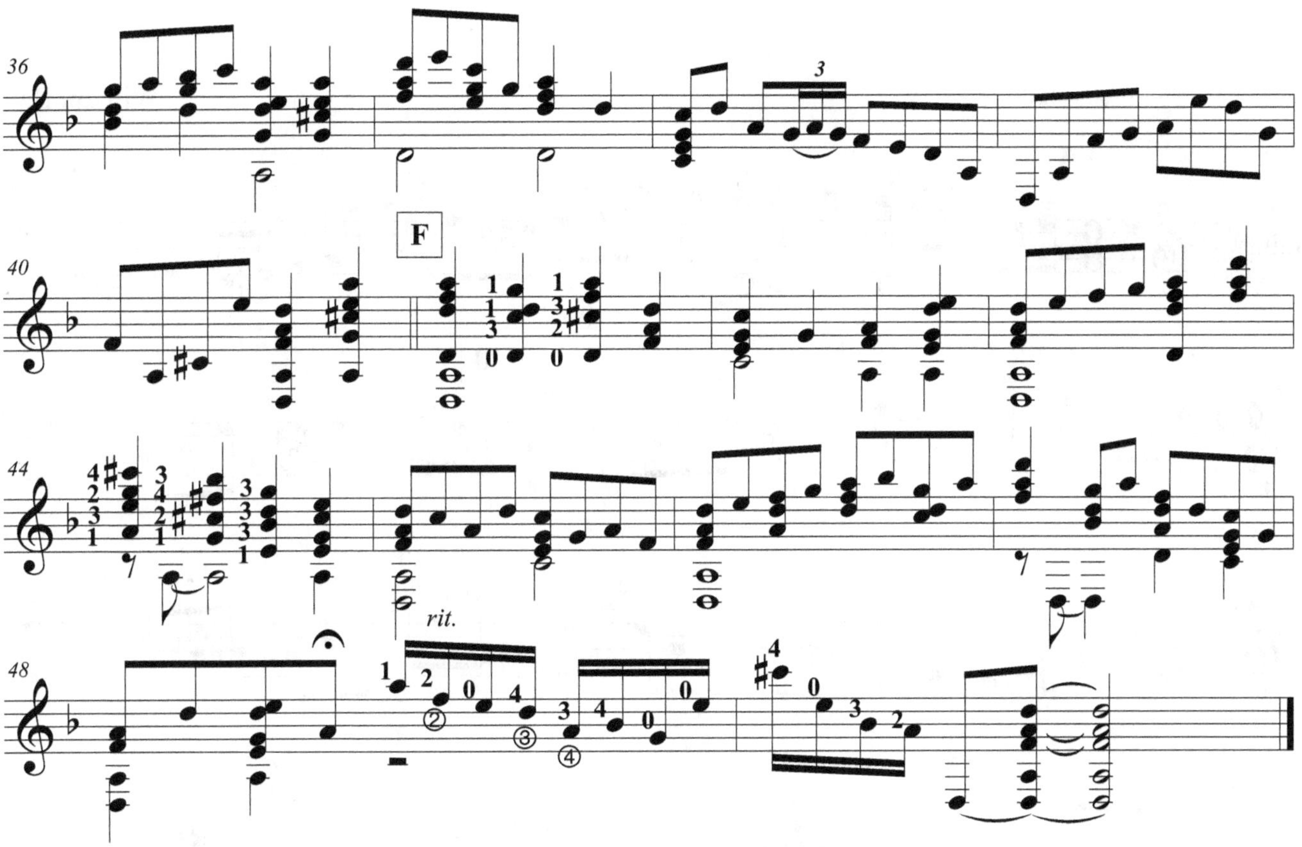
F
rit.

Scherzo

William Bay

F

G

H

I

J

Canticle #2

William Bay

Dolce ♩ = 74

Guitar

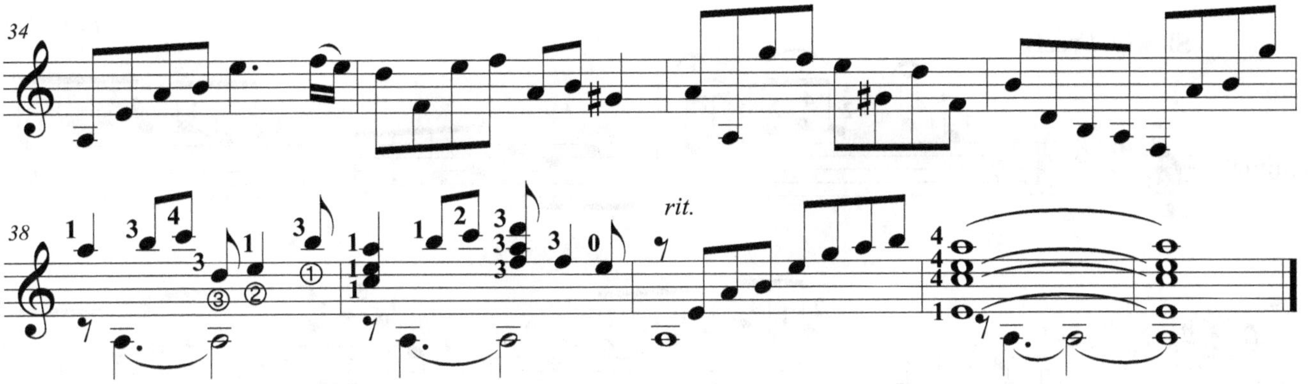
34
38
rit.

Prairie Sunrise

William Bay

Guitar

Slowly, Freely

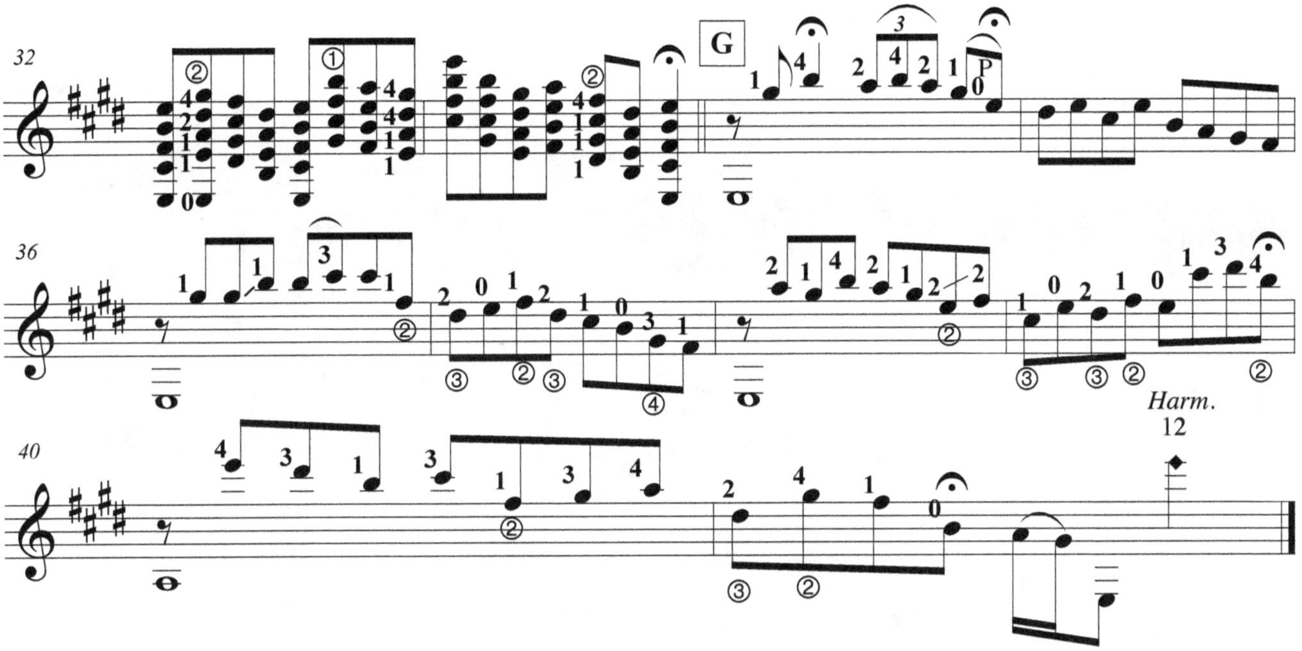
32
G
36
40
Harm.
12

Film Noir

Dropped-D Tuning

Slowly ♩ = 80

William Bay

Meditation on Psalm 13

Flowing tempo, with feeling ♩ = 90

William Bay

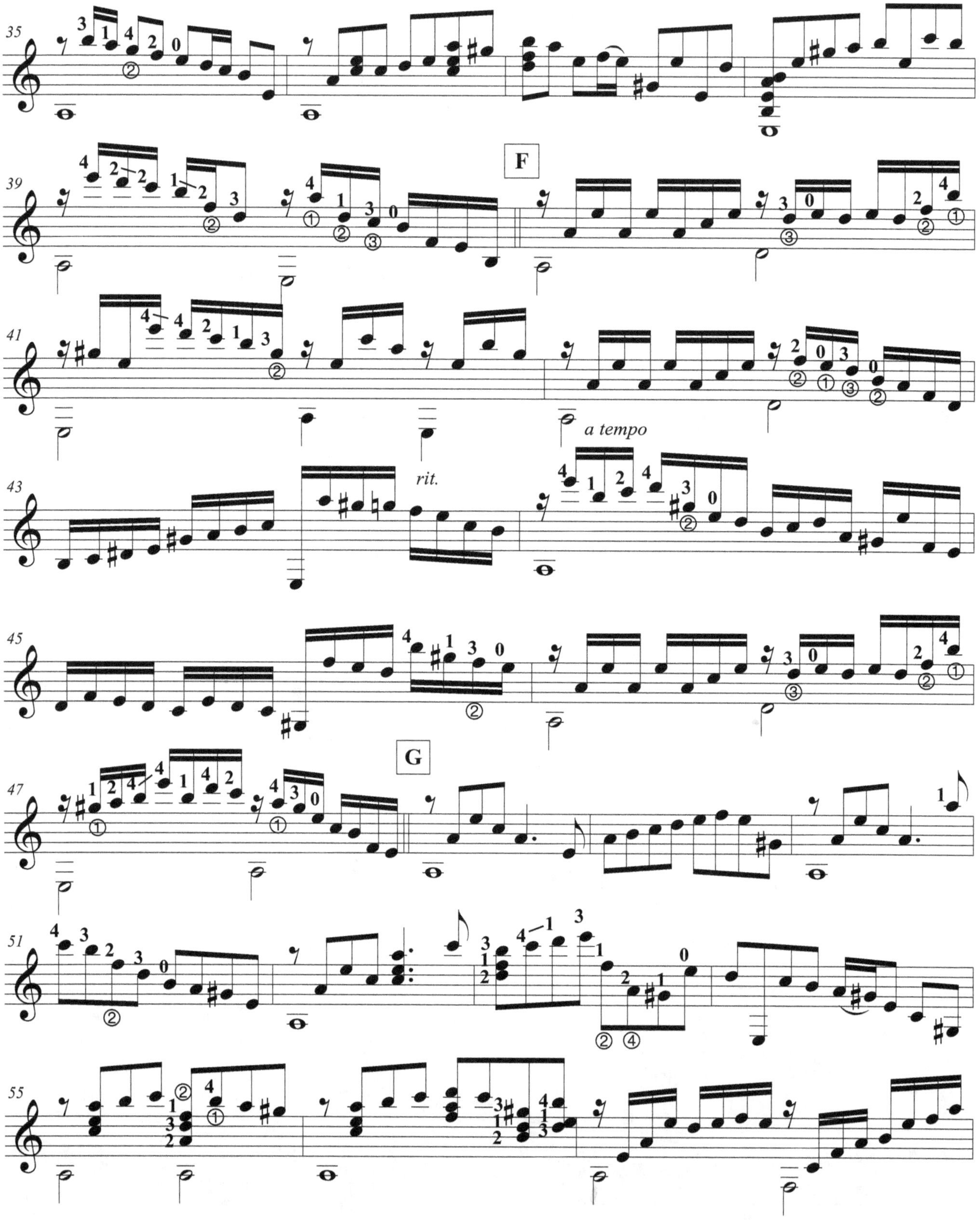
F
a tempo
rit.
G

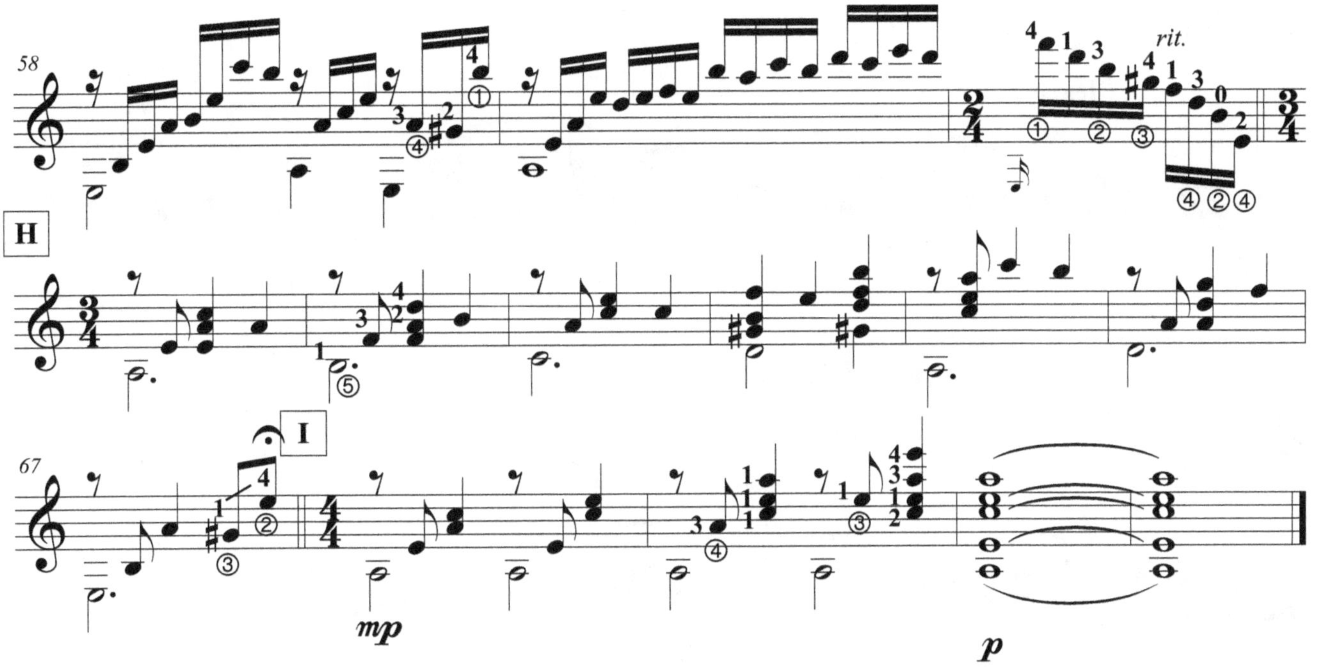
58
rit.
H
67
I
mp
p

Allegro con Spirito
From Sonata #2

Dropped-D Tuning

William Bay

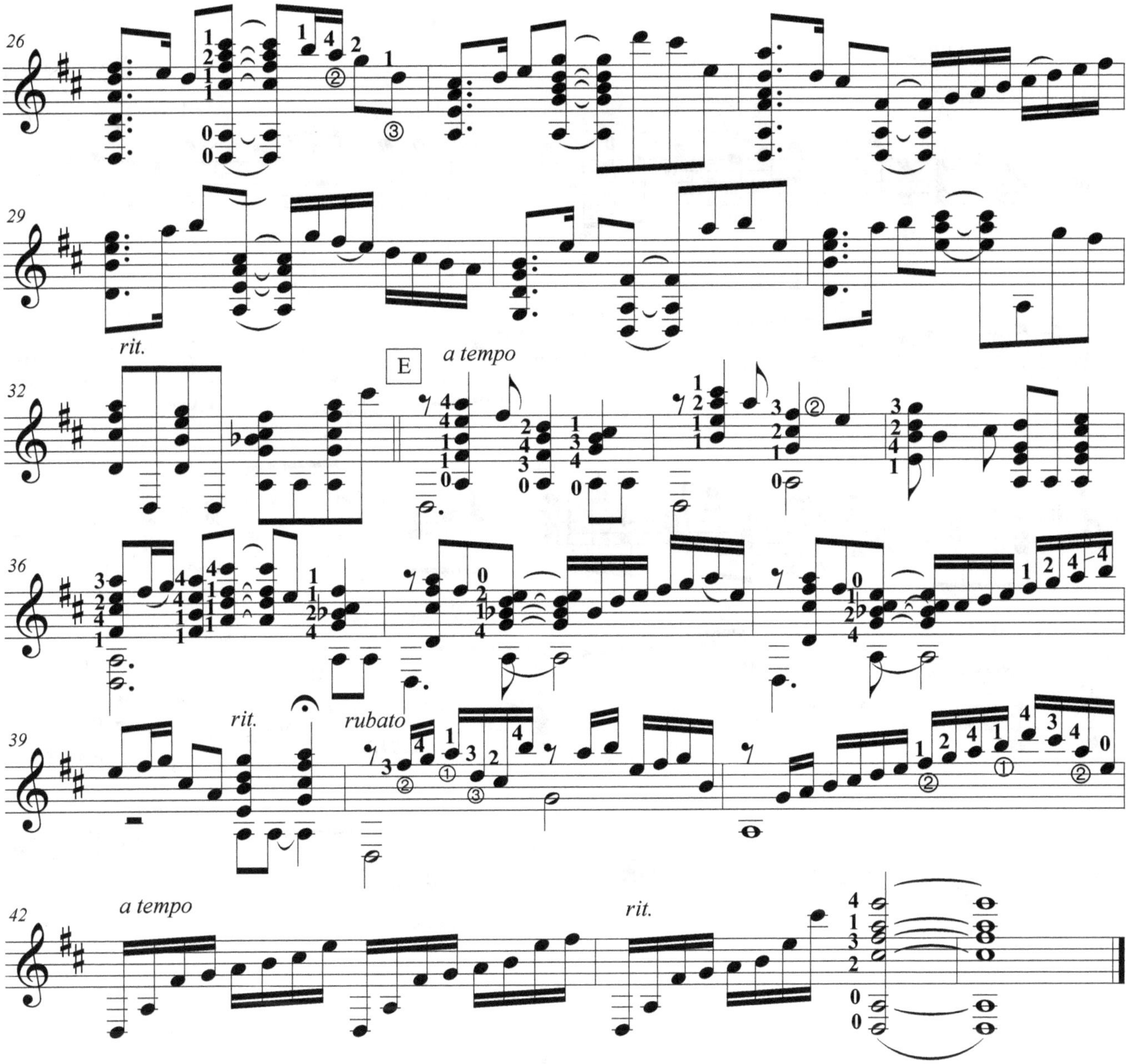
26
29
rit.
32
E
a tempo
36
39
rit.
rubato
42
a tempo
rit.

Lamento para mi madre

Largo ♩ = 60

William Bay

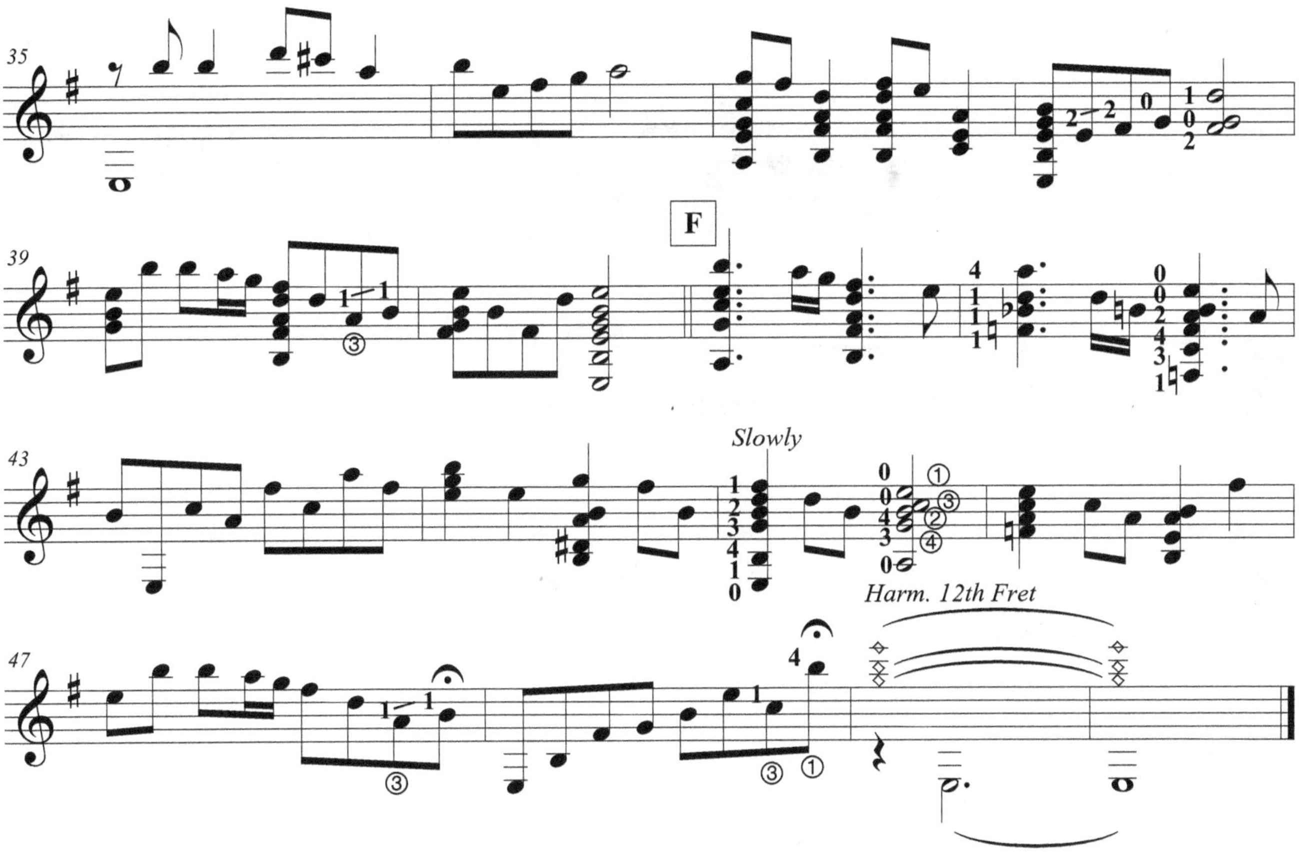
F
Slowly
Harm. 12th Fret

Prayer

Rubato ♩ = 80

William Bay

Guitar

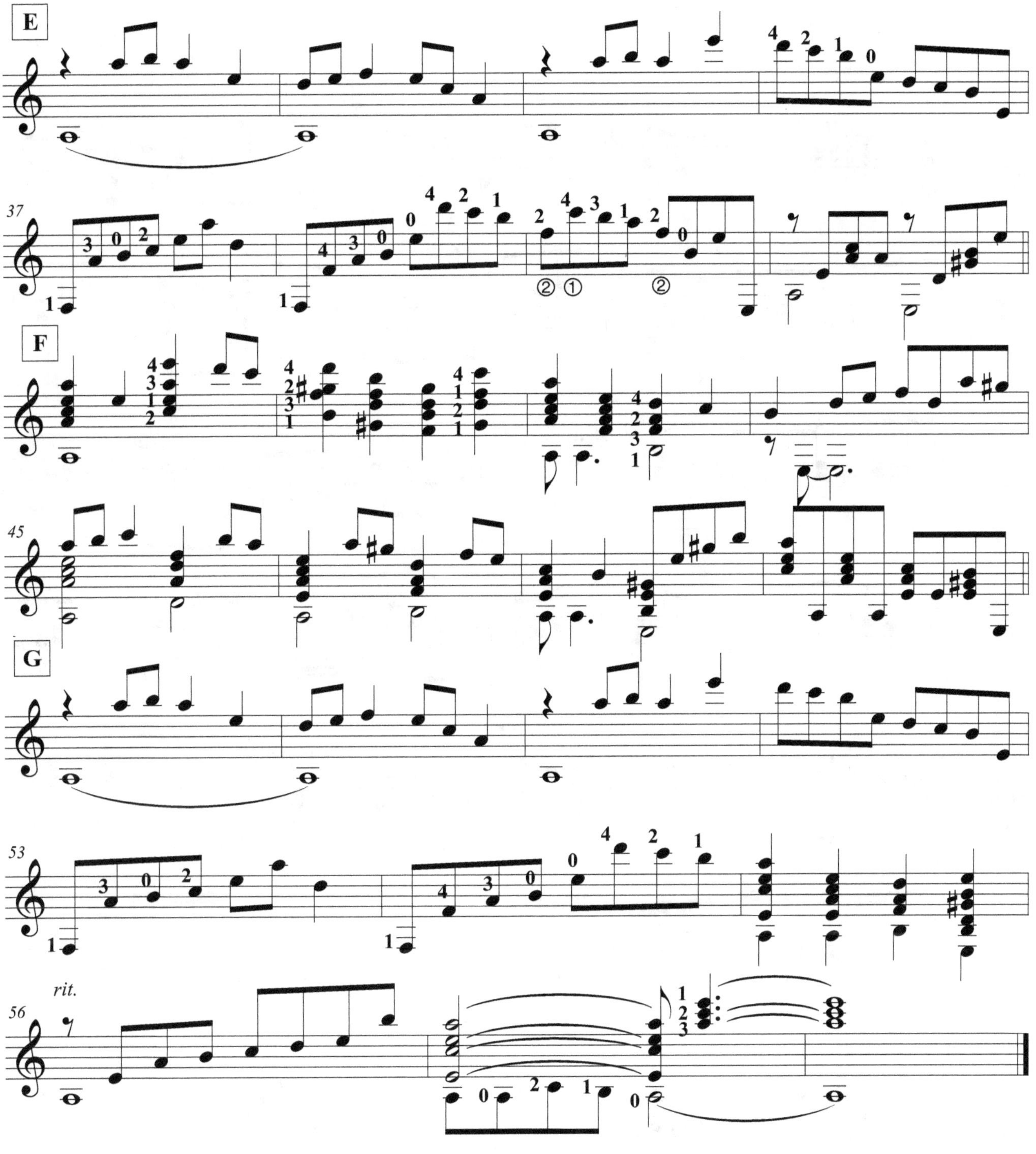
E
37
F
45
G
53
56
rit.

Nocturne #3

Dropped-D Tuning

William Bay

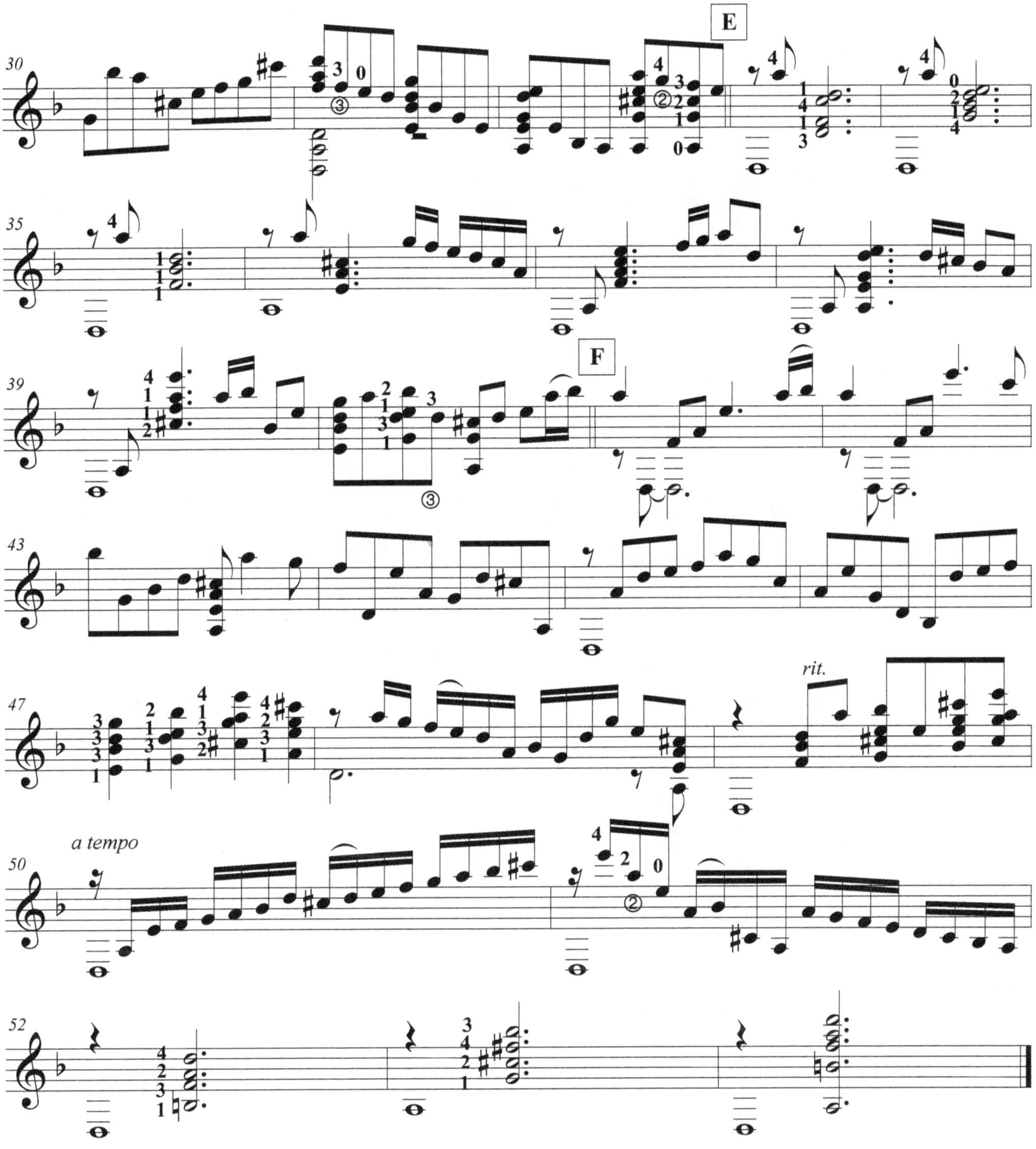
E
F
rit.
a tempo

Tango #3

Dropped-D Tuning

Allegretto ♩ = 120

William Bay

Guitar

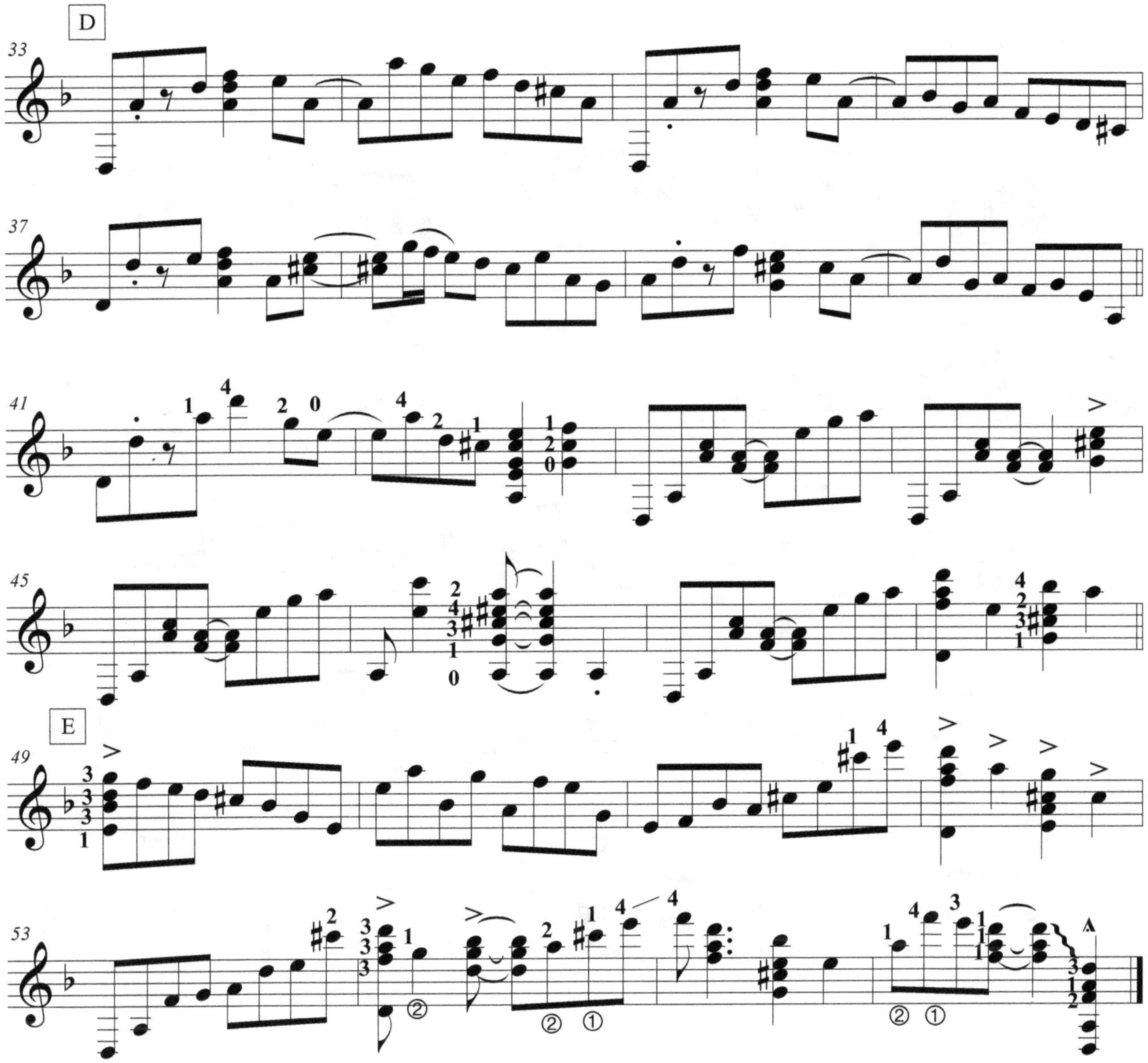
D
33
37
41
45
E
49
53

Meditation on Psalm 40

Dropped D Tuning

William Bay

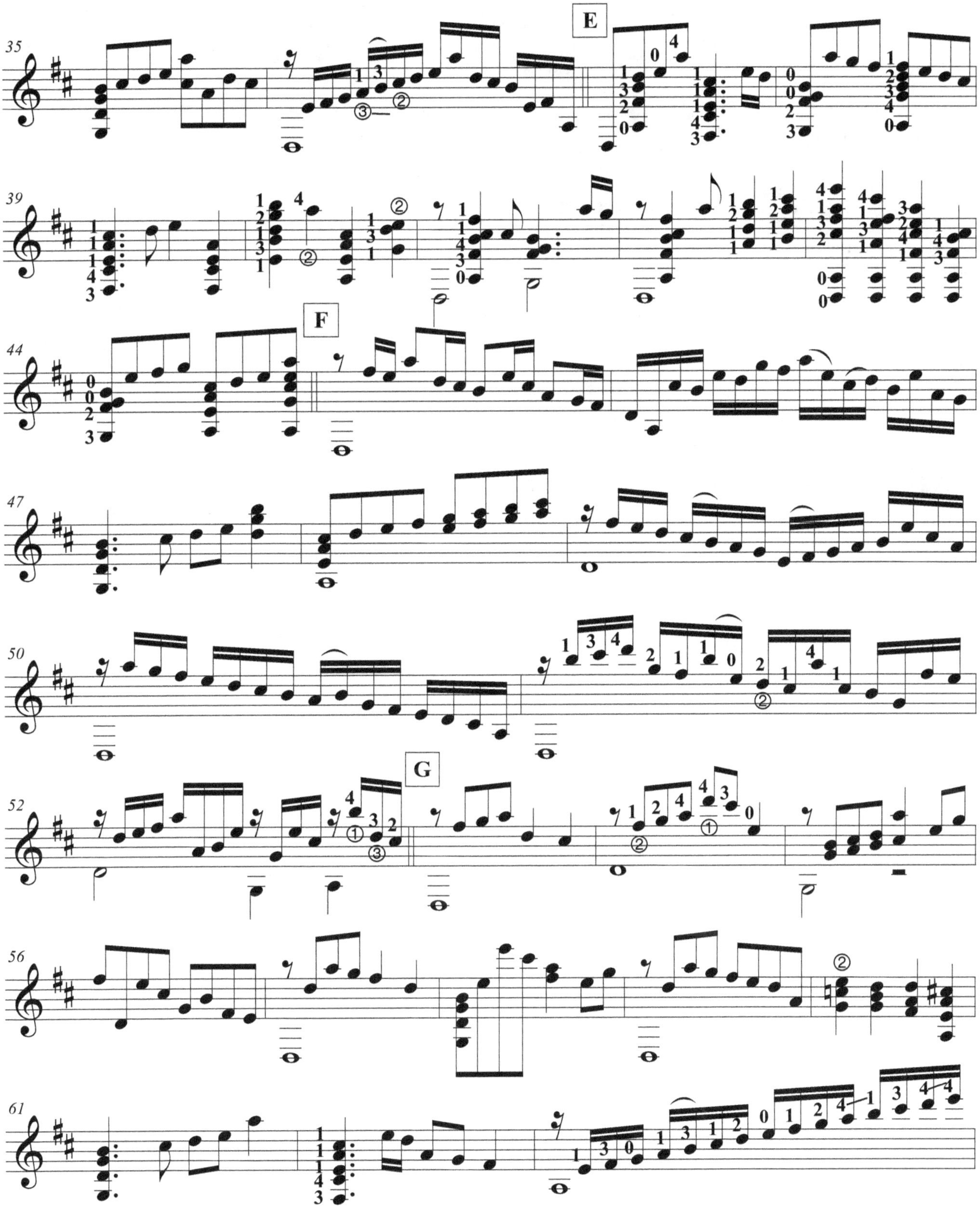
E
F
G

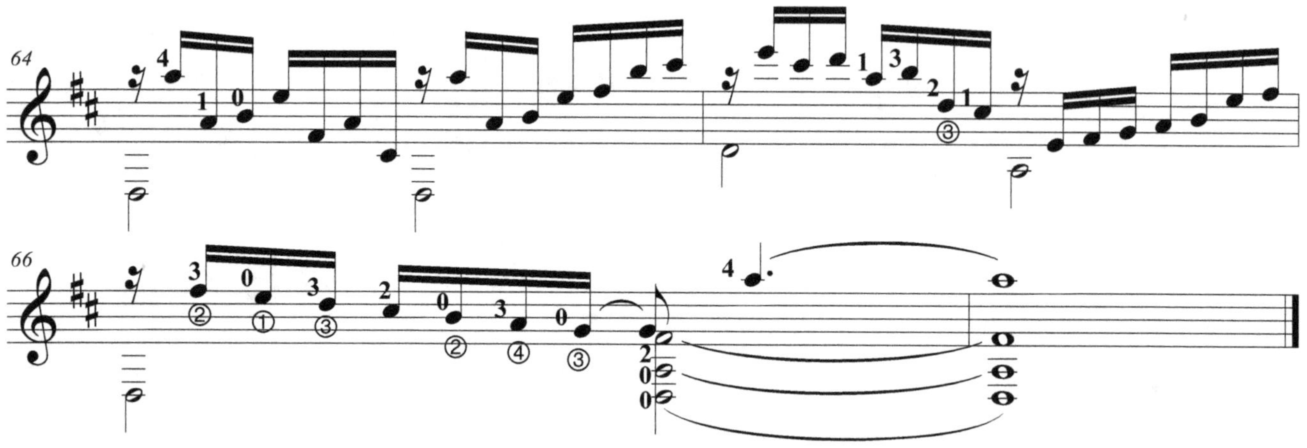
64
66

Irish Prayer

Dropped-D Tuning

Peacefully ♩ = 80

William Bay

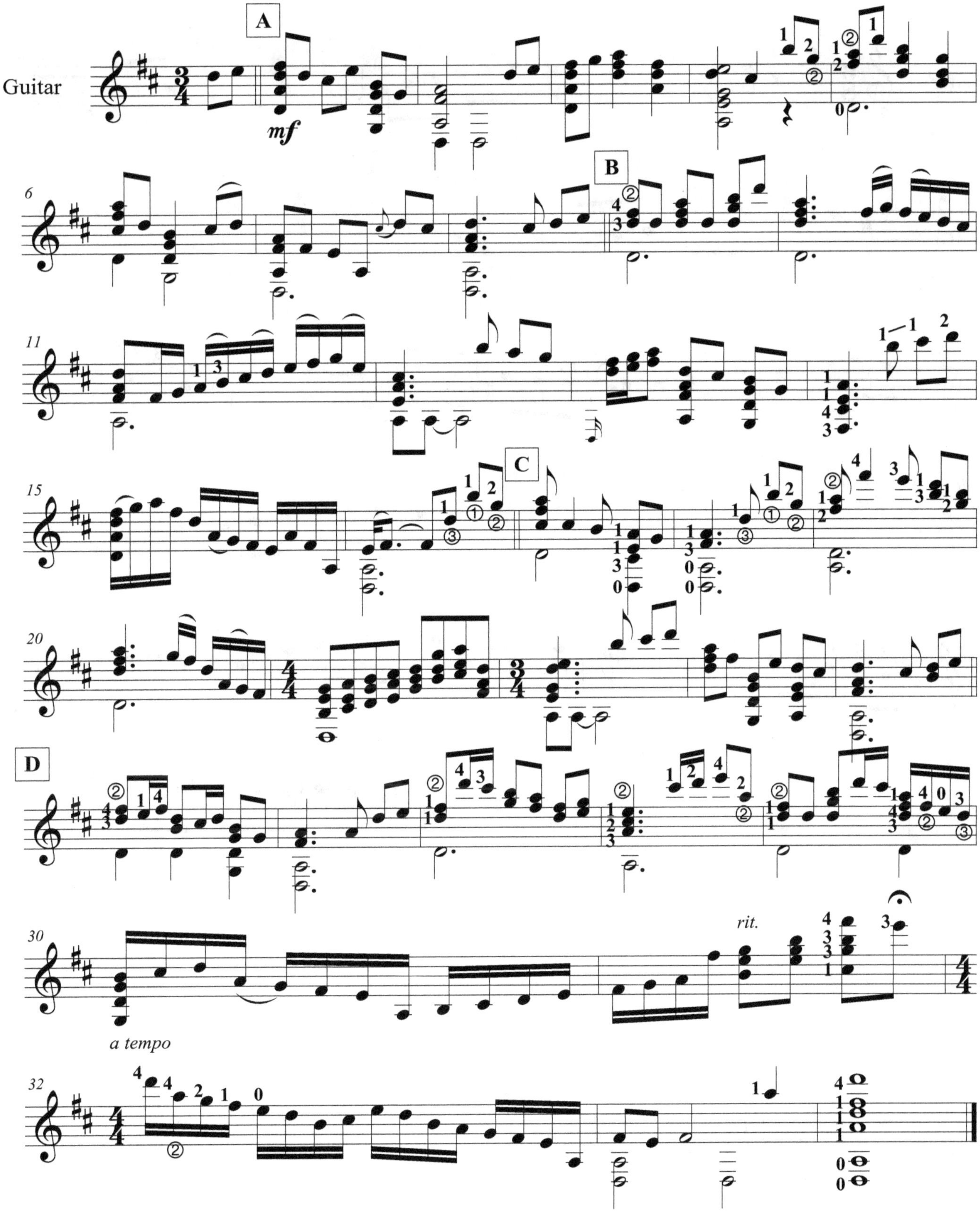

Tarantella

William Bay

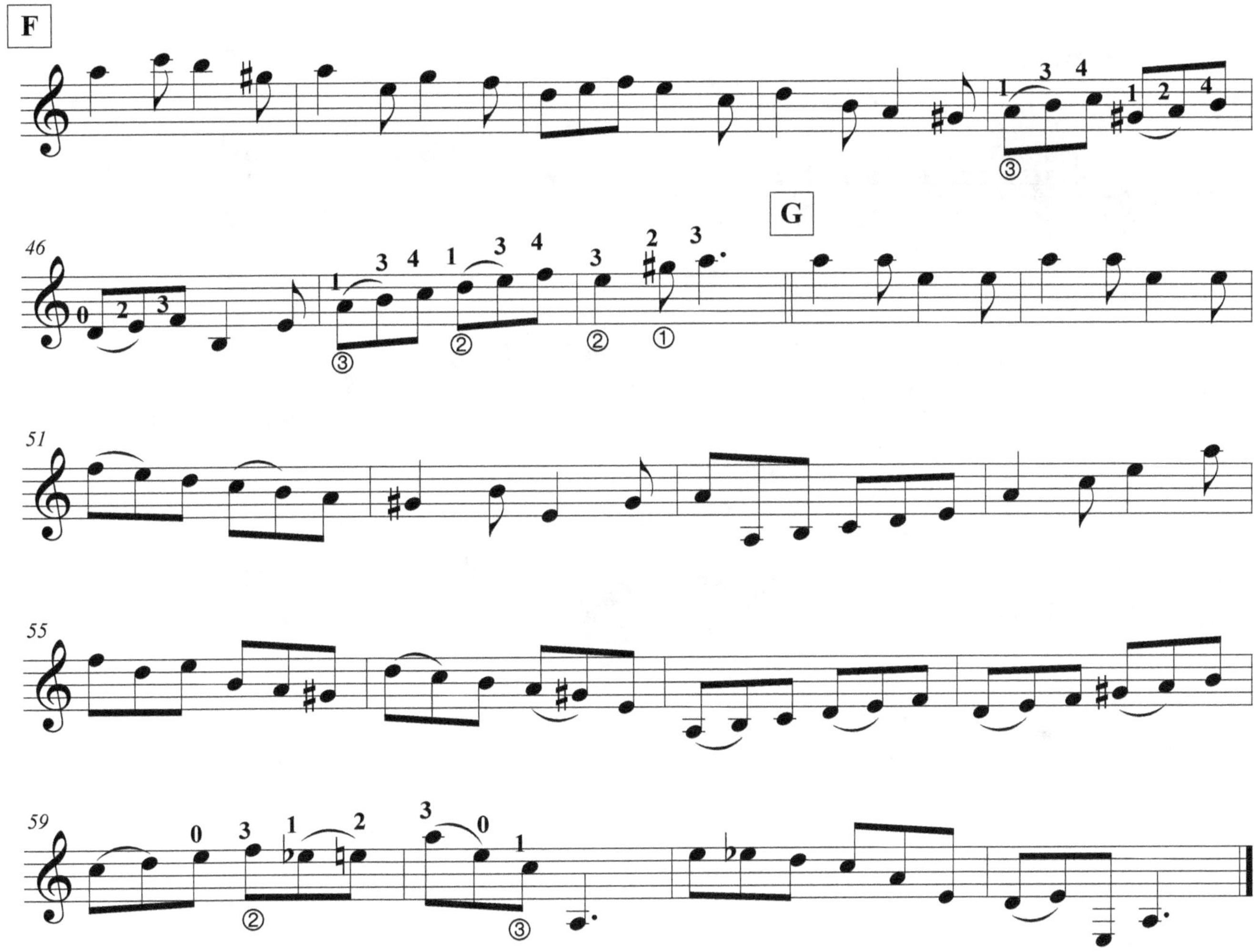
F
46
G
51
55
59

Communion

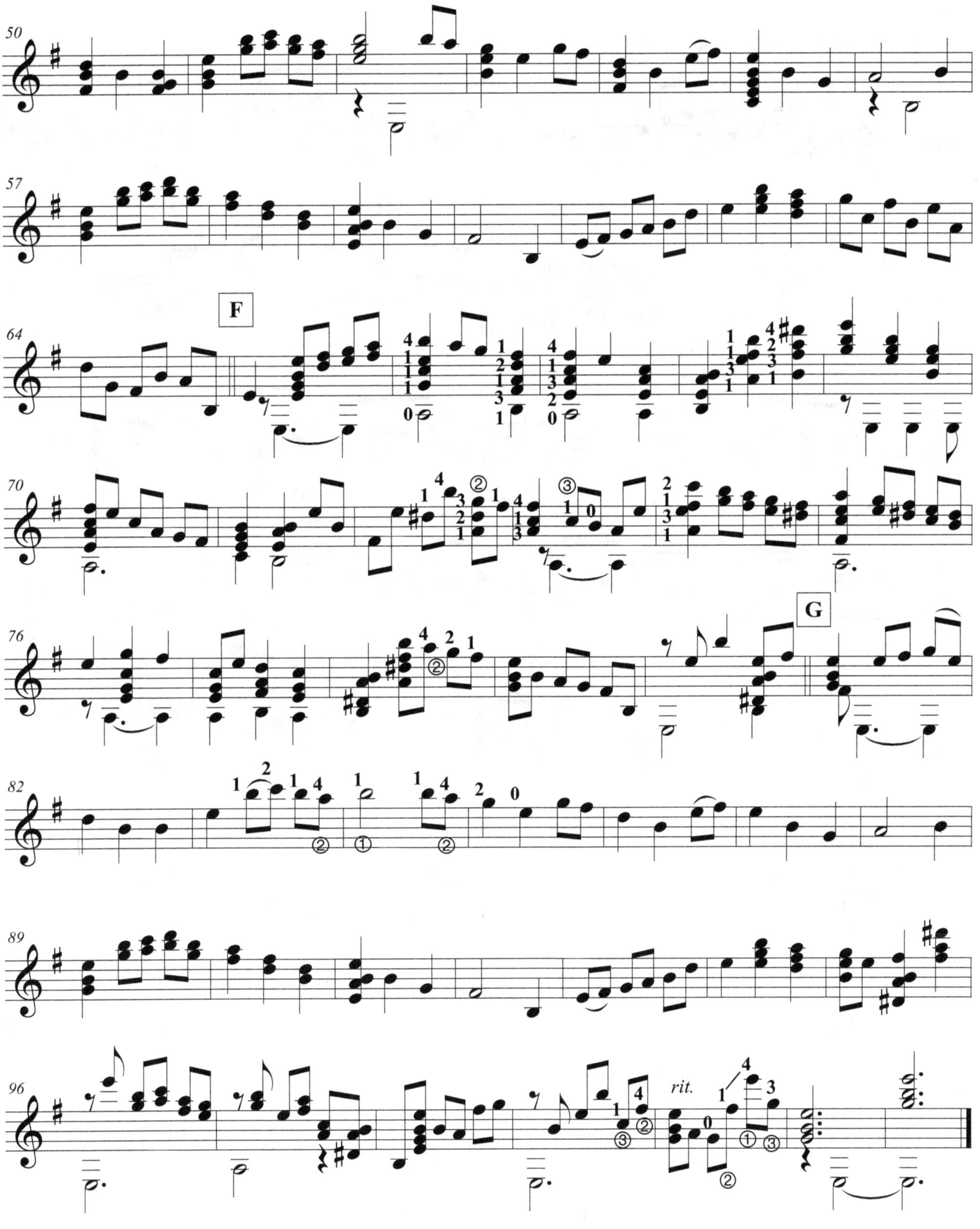
50
57
64
F
70
76
G
82
89
96
rit.

Meditation on Psalm 92

Dropped-D Tuning

Slowly, with Expression ♩ = 72

William Bay

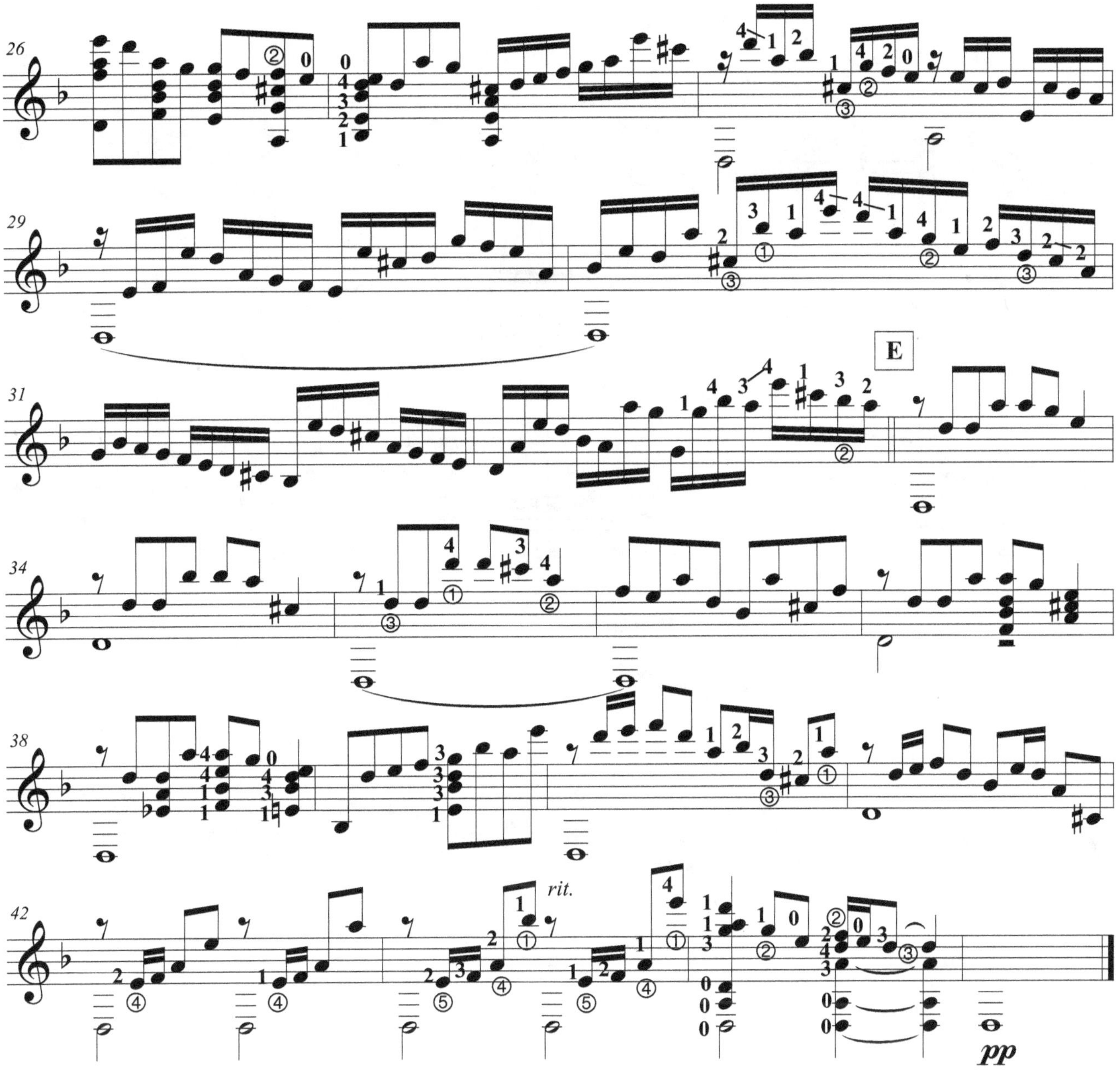
26
29
31
E
34
38
42
rit.
pp

Allegro
From Sonata #2

Dropped-D Tuning

Joyfully ♩. = 68

William Bay

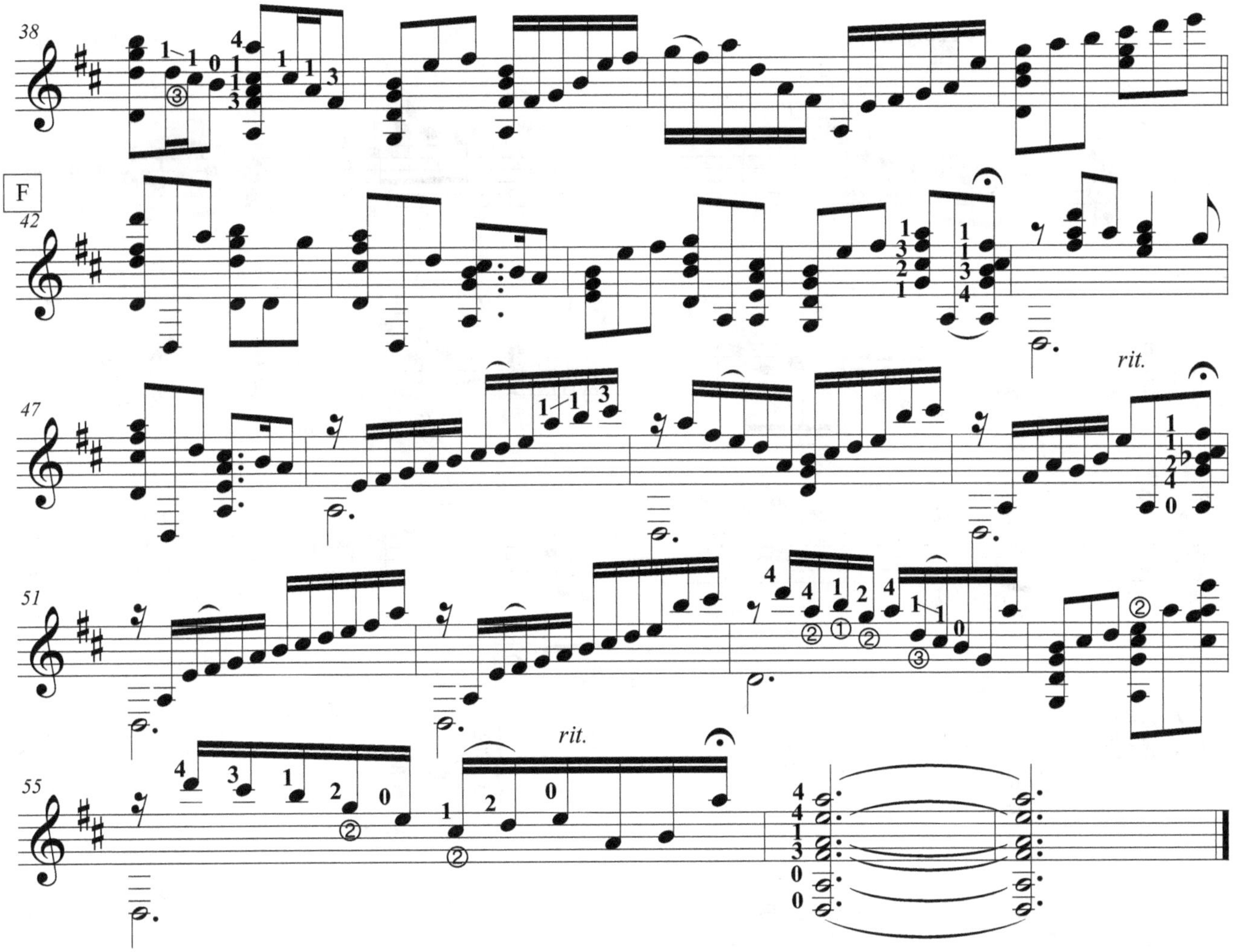
F
rit.
rit.

Longing

Adagio, Freely ♩ = 66

William Bay

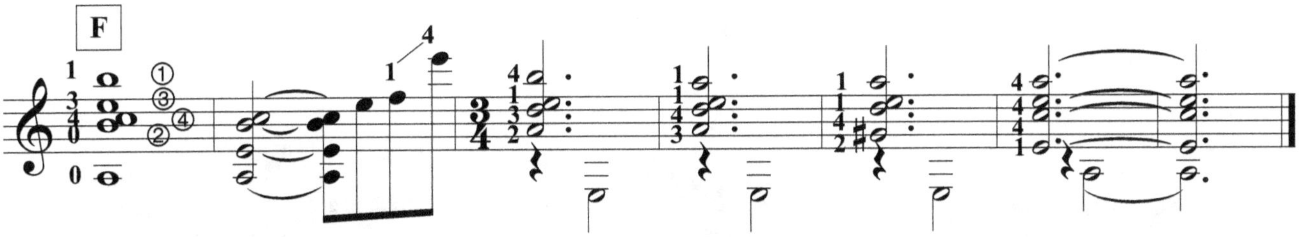
F

Regret

Dolce, Very Freely

William Bay

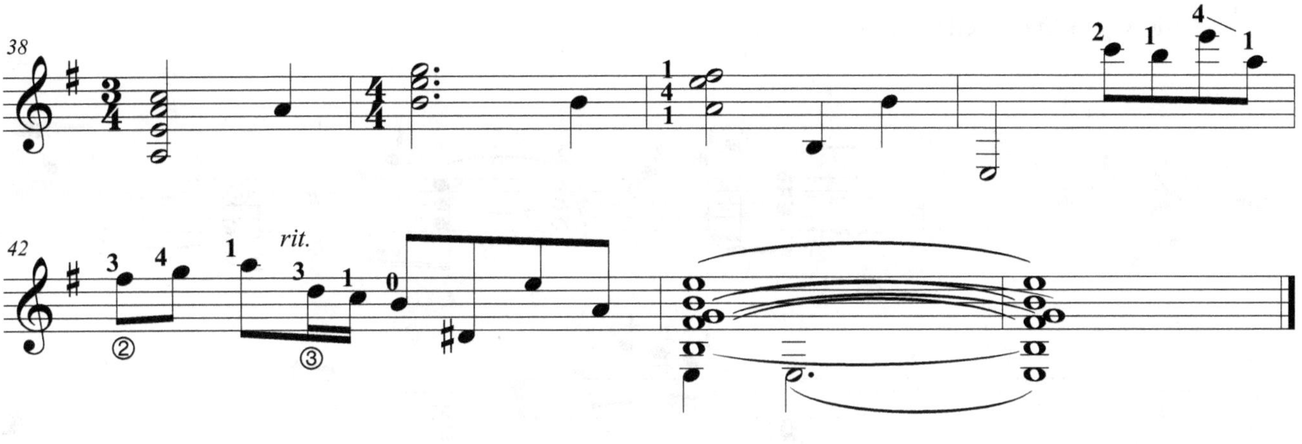
38
42
rit.

Vigil

Slowly, With Feeling ♩ = 68

William Bay

Guitar

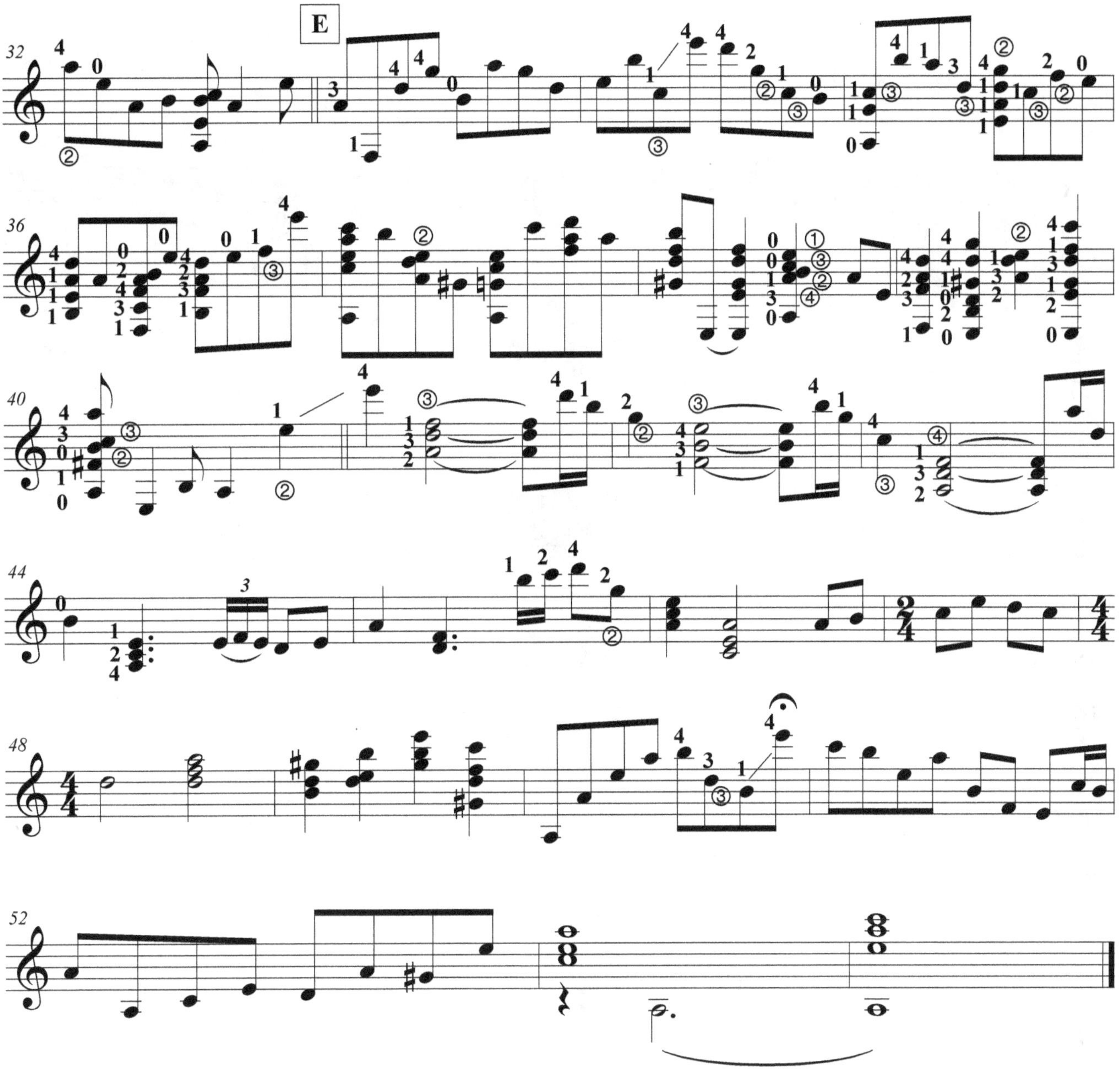
E

Tango #12

William Bay

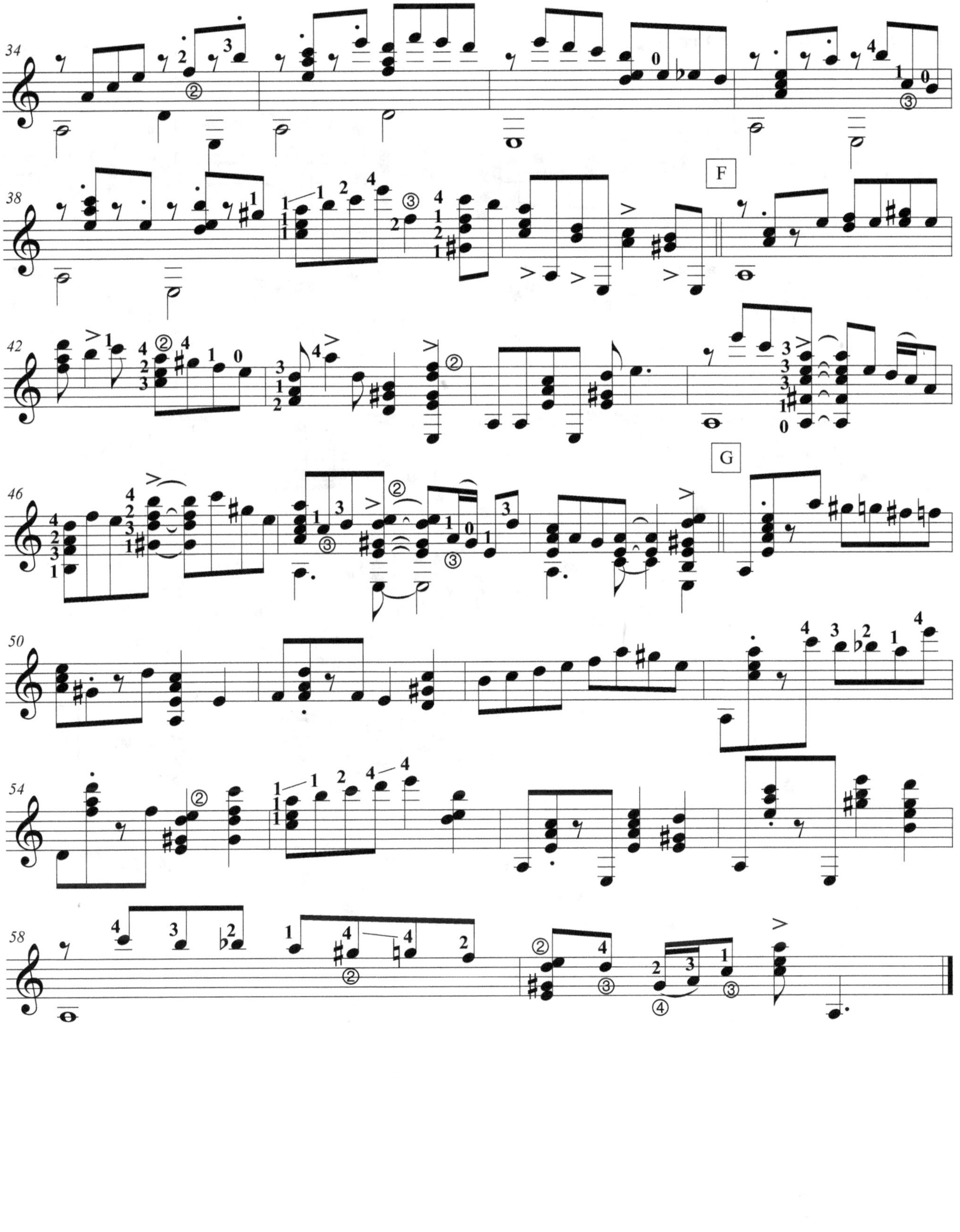
F
G

Contemplation

Rubato, Slowly and Freely ♩ = 68

William Bay

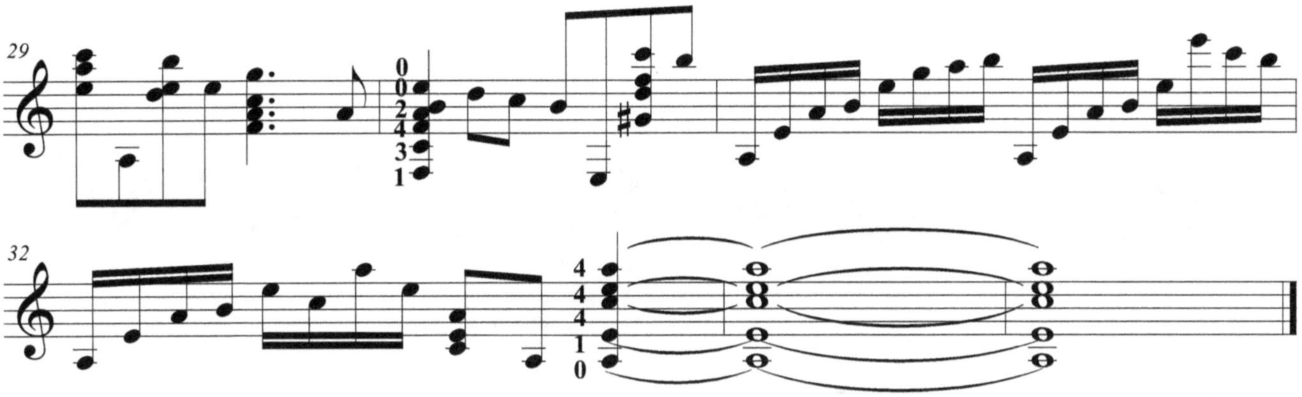
29
32

Meditation on Psalm 116

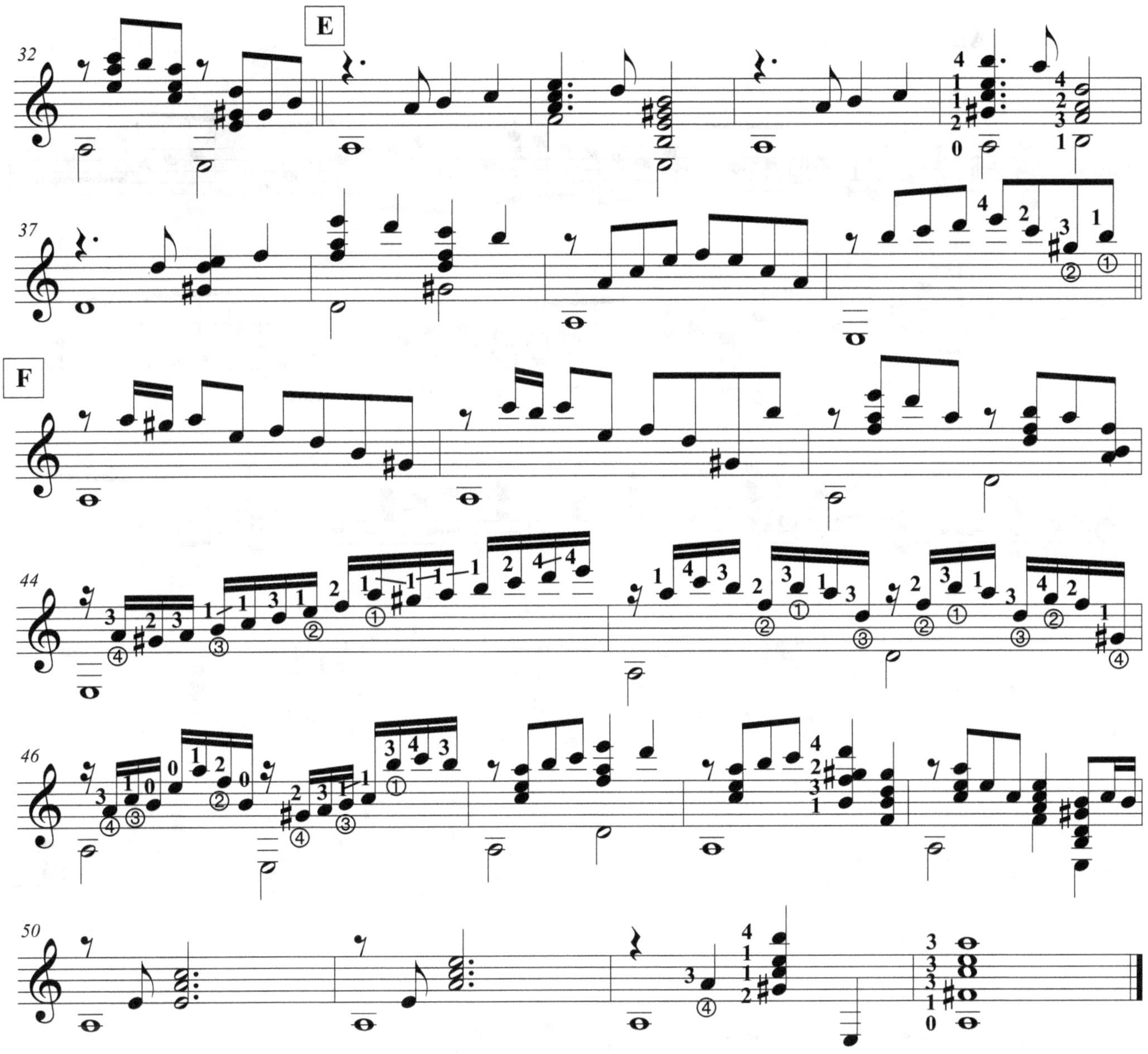
E
F

Invention
In C Minor

Allegro ♩ = 100

William Bay

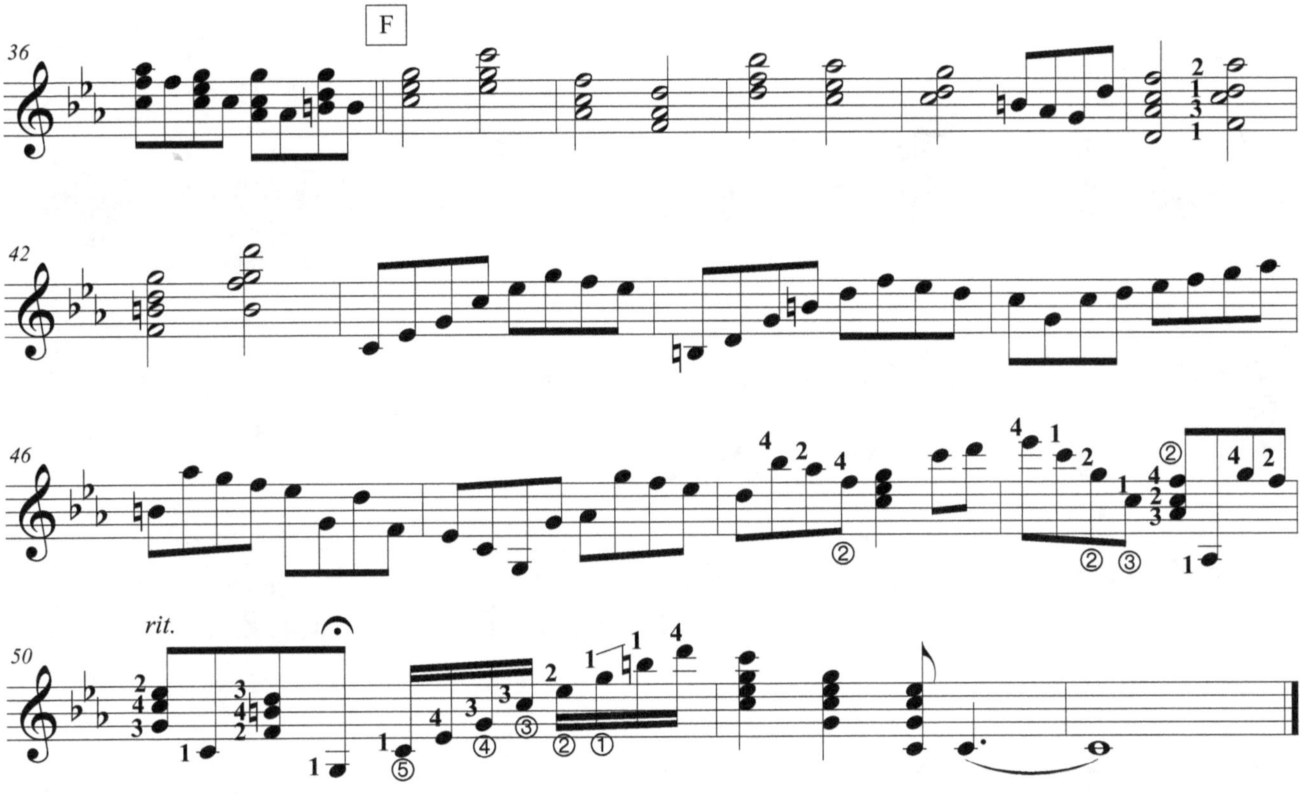
36
F
42
46
50
rit.

Allegro
From Sonata #3

William Bay

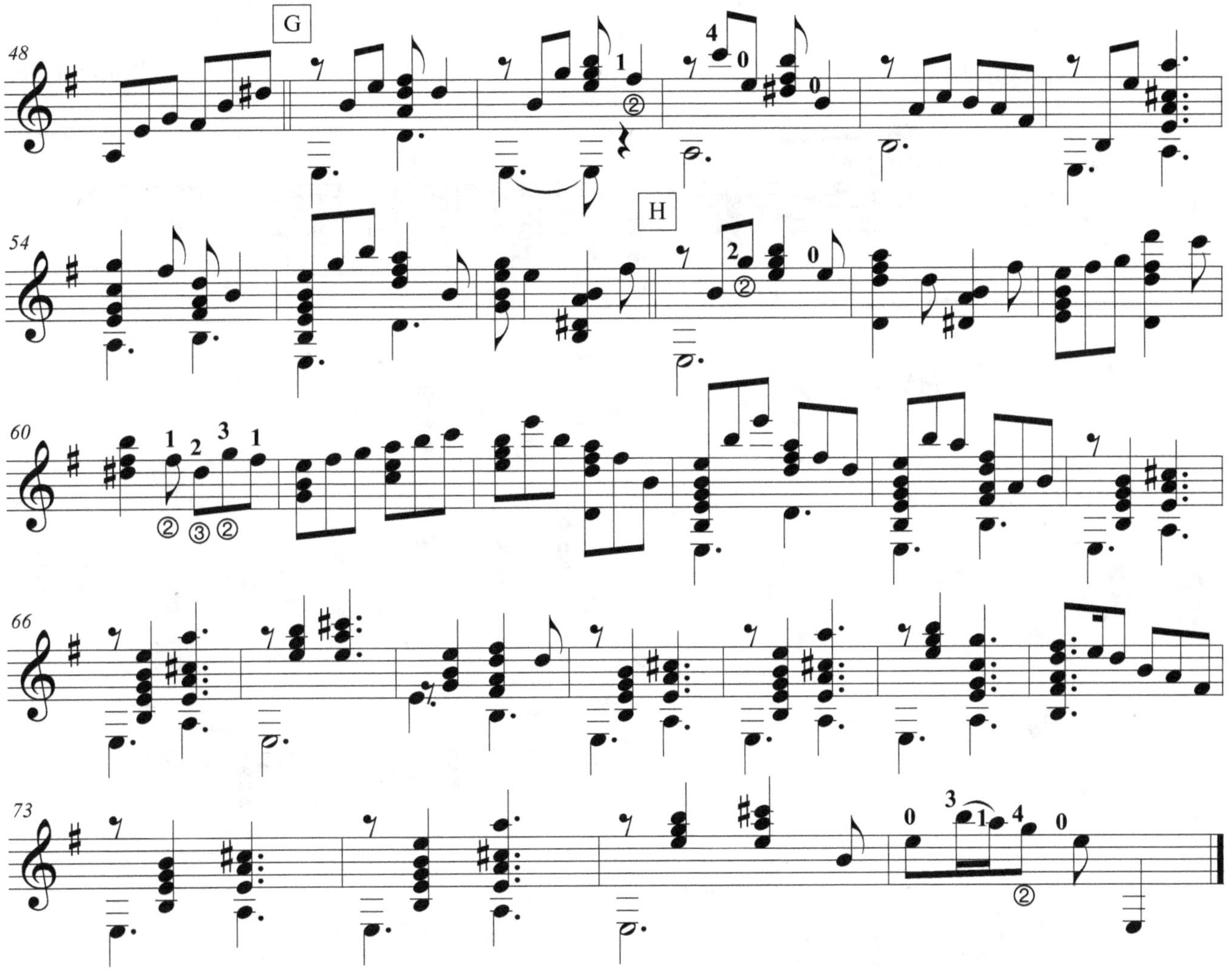
G
H

Adagio

Dropped-D Tuning

William Bay

Adagio ♩ = 66

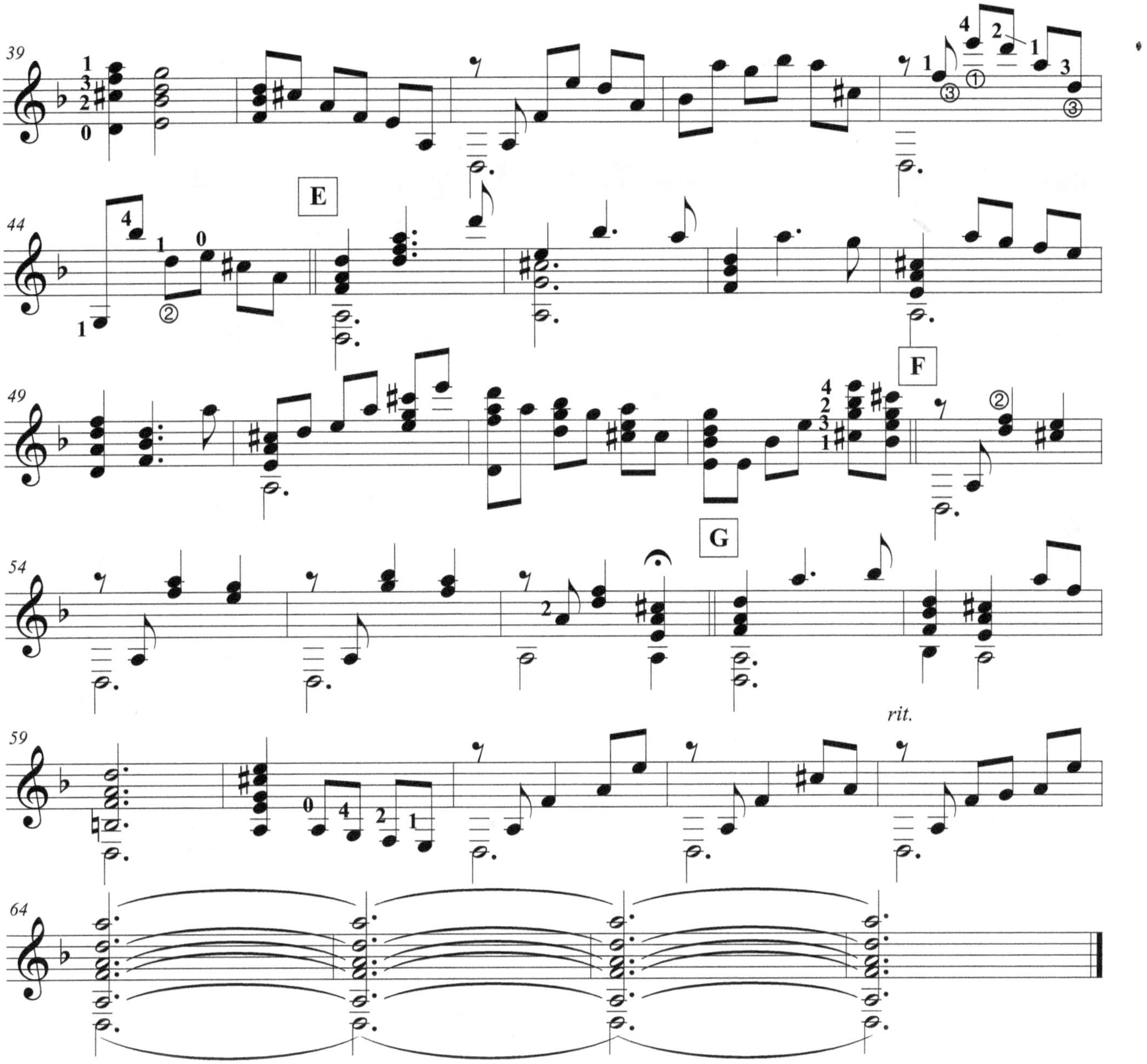
39
44
E
49
F
54
G
rit.
59
64

Alone

Andante Cantabile ♩ = 68

William Bay

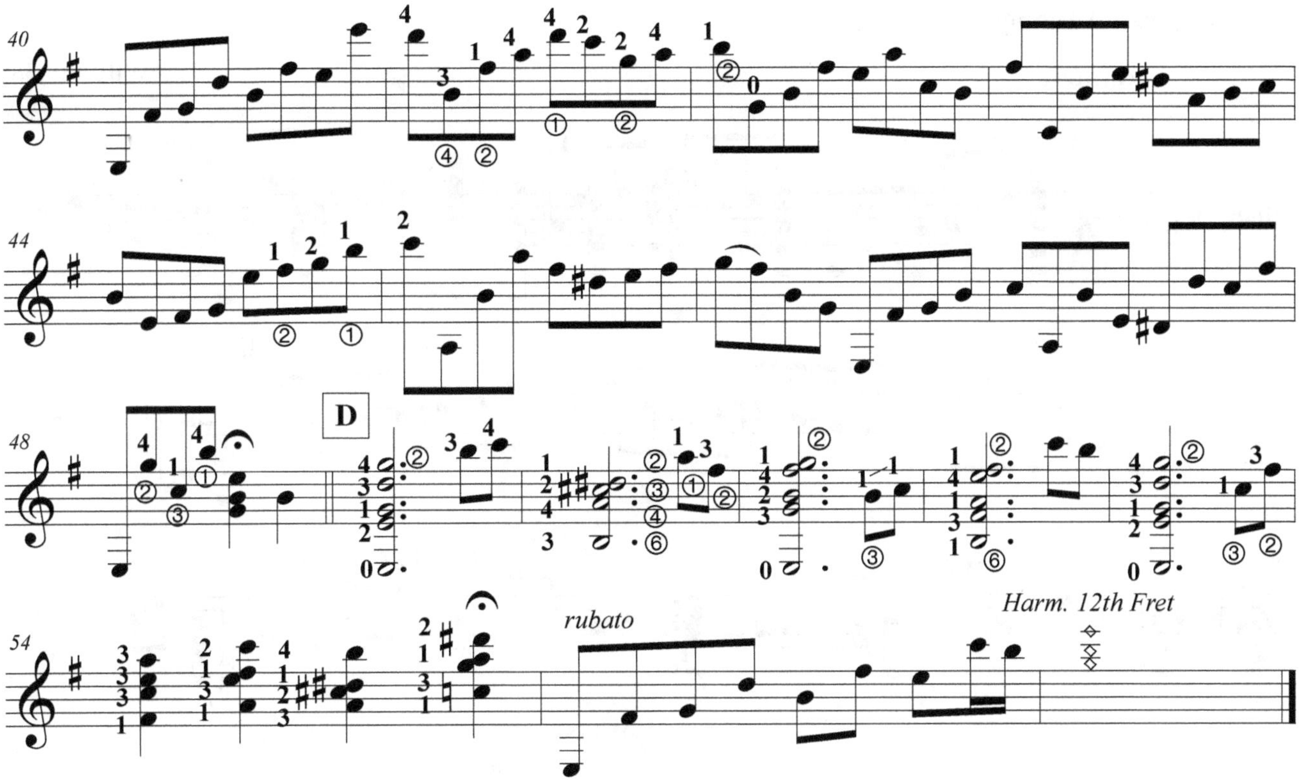
40
44
48
D
54
rubato
Harm. 12th Fret

Prayer #2

Dropped-D Tuning

Andante ♩ = 72

William Bay

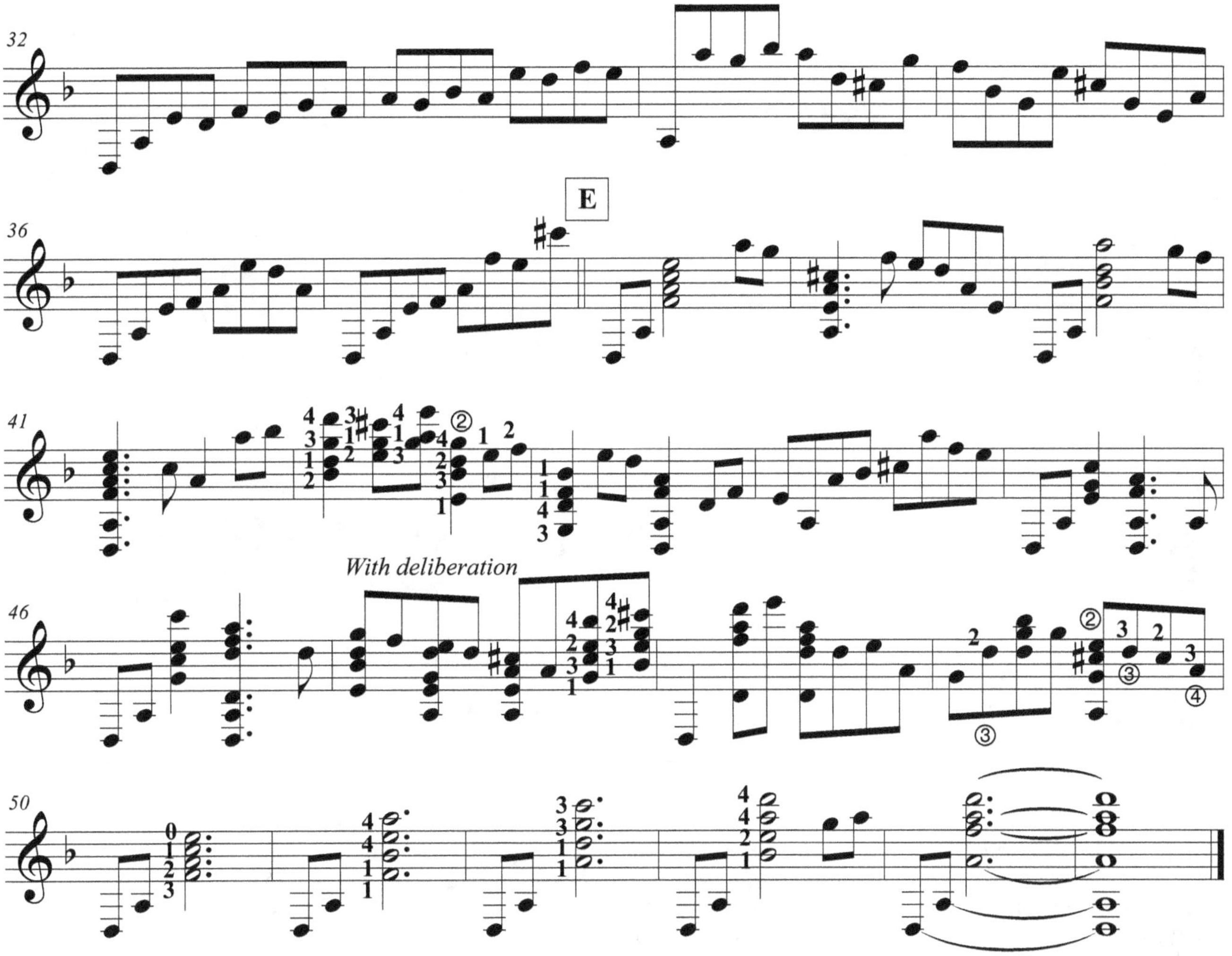
32
36
E
41
With deliberation
46
50

Sanctuary

William Bay

Harmonic 12th Fret

pp

Song

Gently ♩ = 90

William Bay

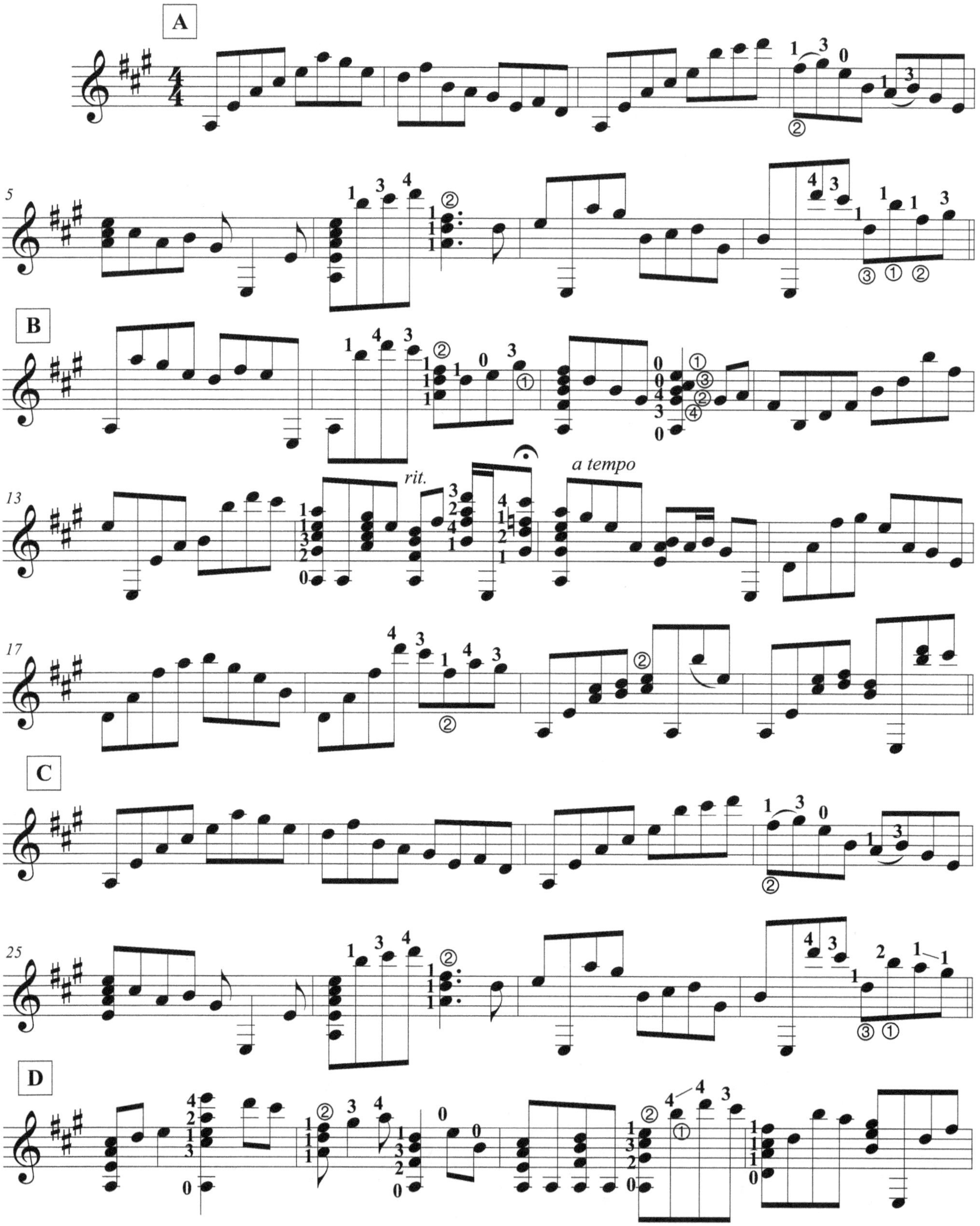

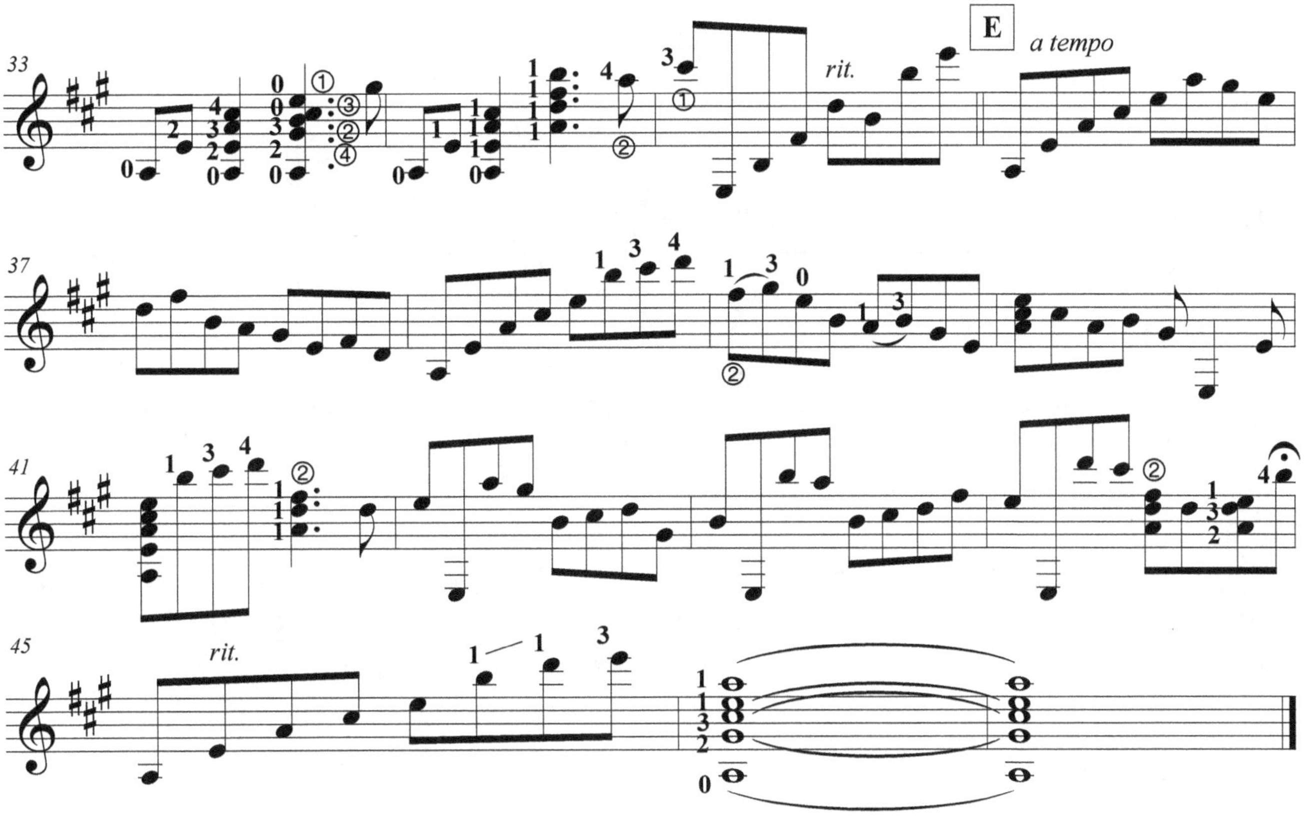
E
a tempo
rit.
rit.

A Brighter Day Will Come

Dropped-D Tuning

Gently ♩ = 74

William Bay

Guitar

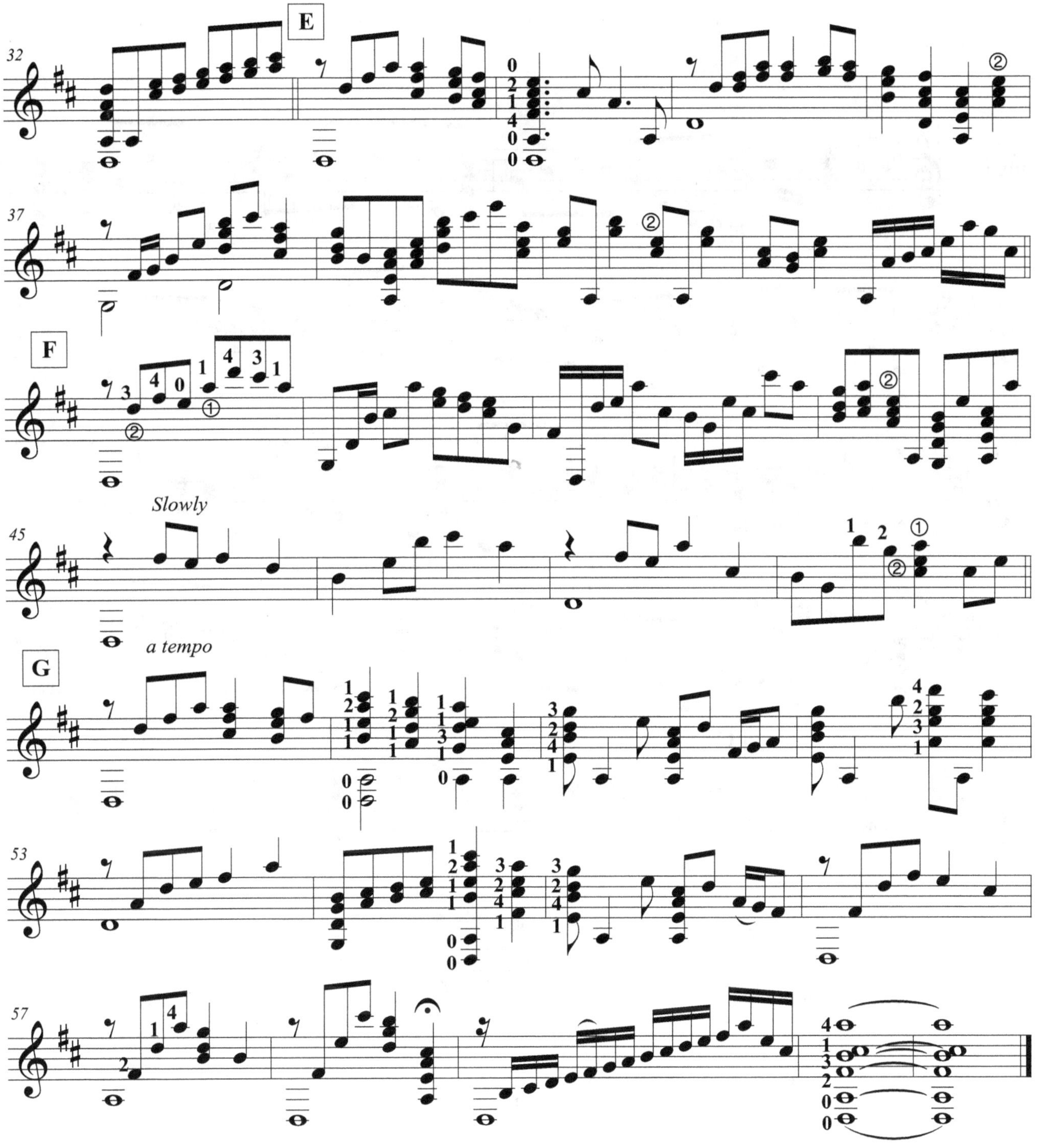
E
F
Slowly
a tempo
G

Sunrise

William Bay

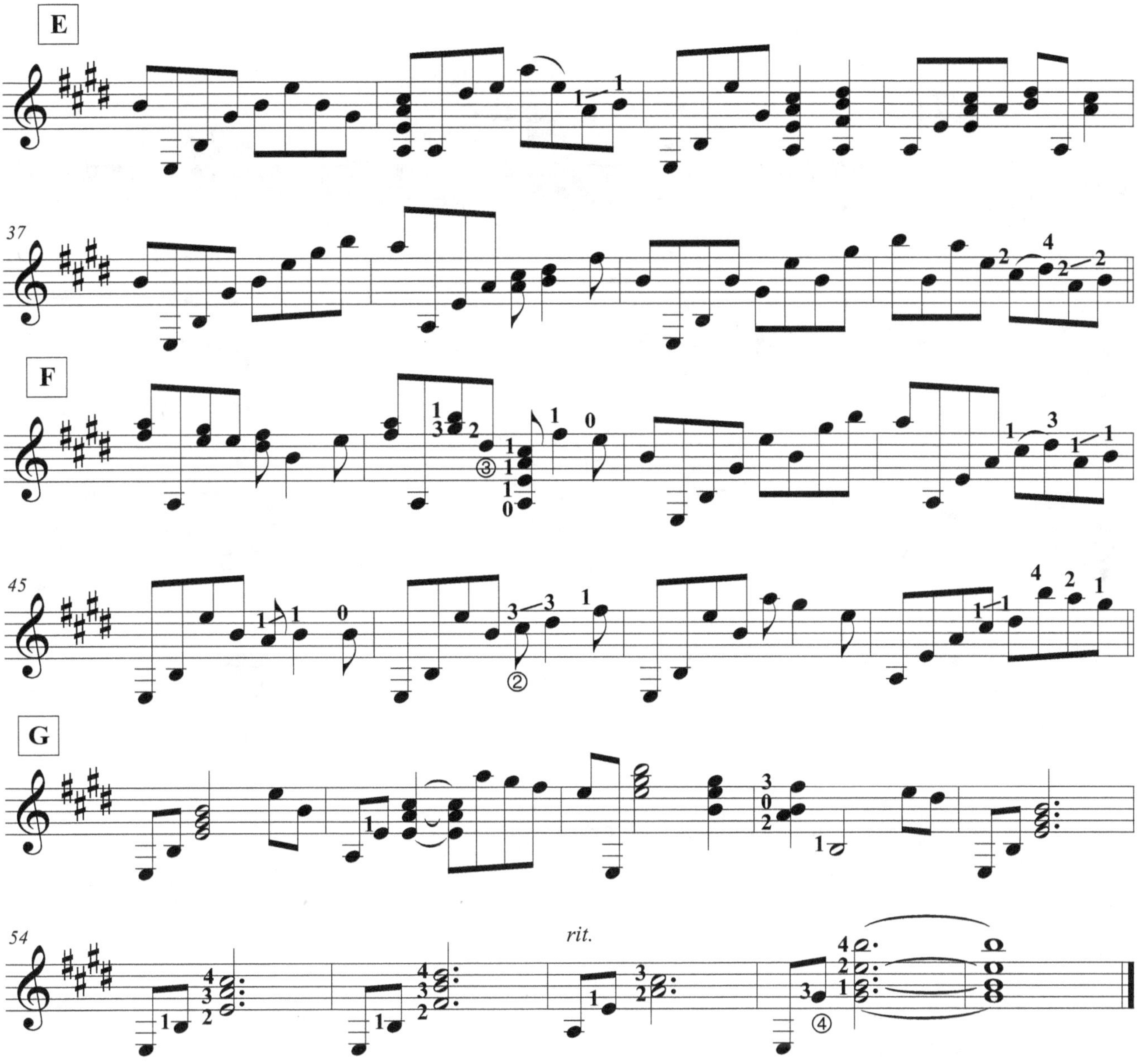
E
37
F
45
G
54
rit.

New Beginnings

Dropped-D Tuning

Lyrically ♩ = 78

William Bay

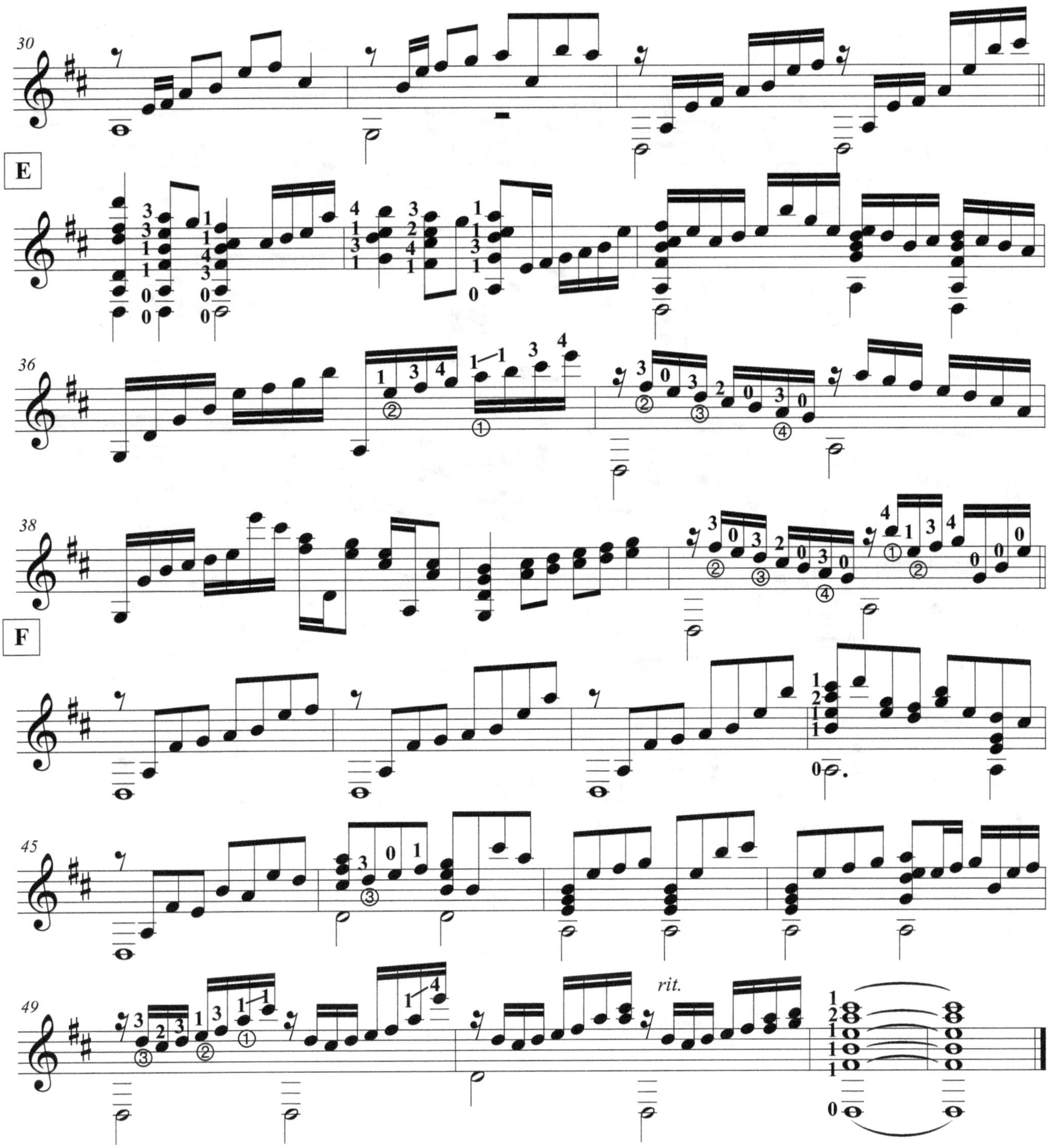
30
E
36
38
F
45
49
rit.

Prelude #1

Moderato ♩. = 60

William Bay

Guitar

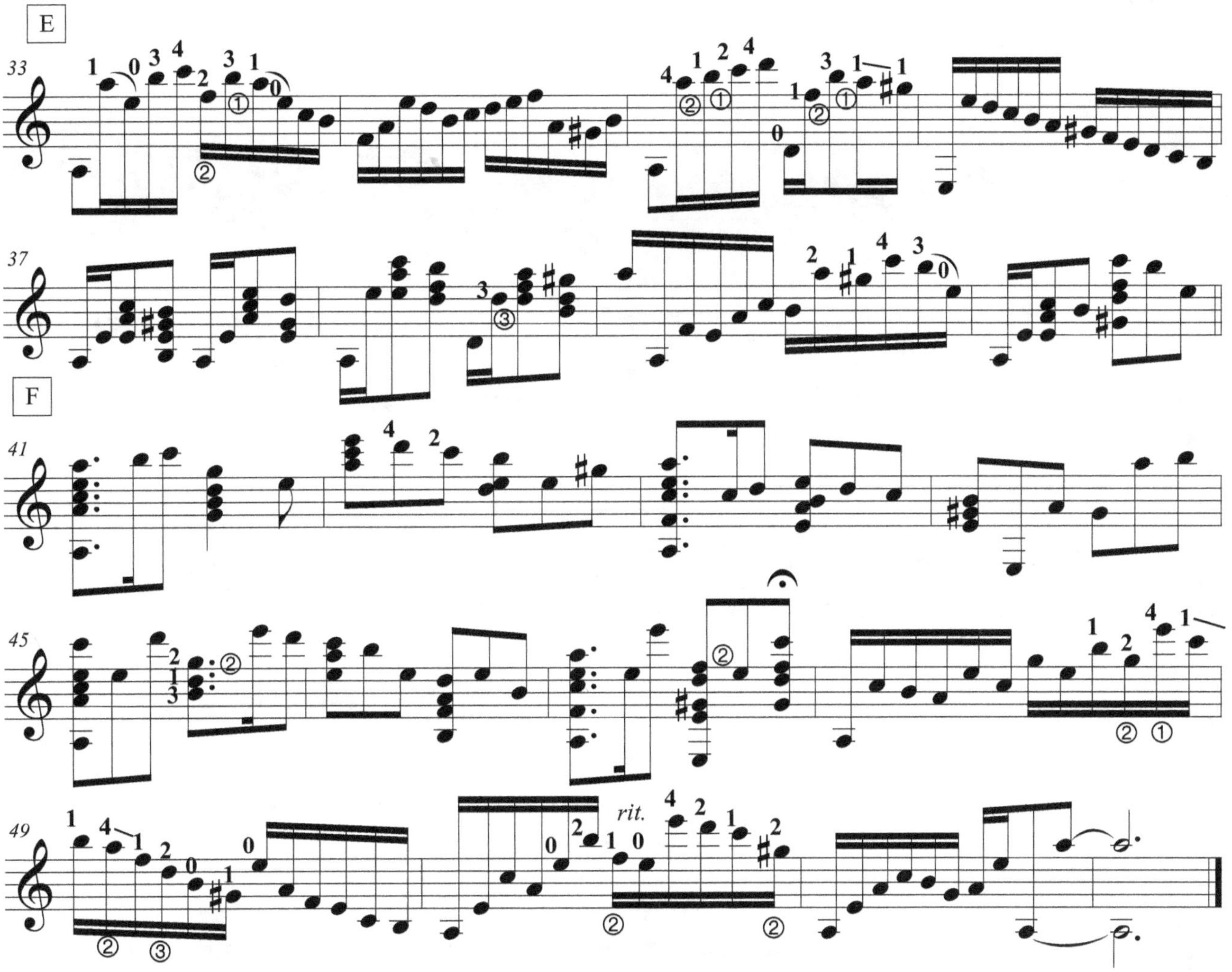
E
33
37
F
41
45
49
rit.

Prelude #3

Dropped-D Tuning

Boldly ♩ = 76

William Bay

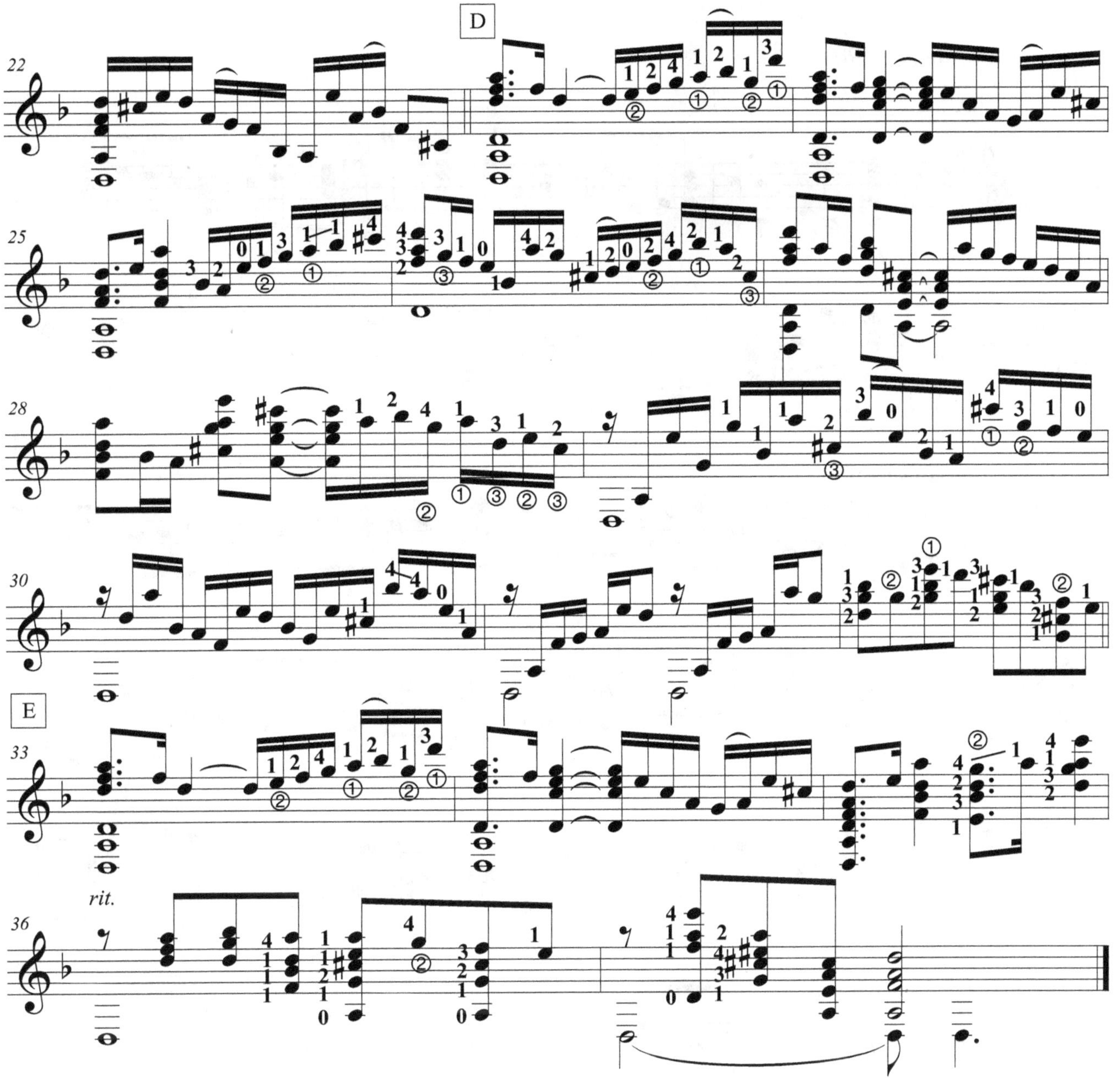
D
E
rit.

Prelude #5

Andante ($\quad$ = 90)

William Bay

Guitar

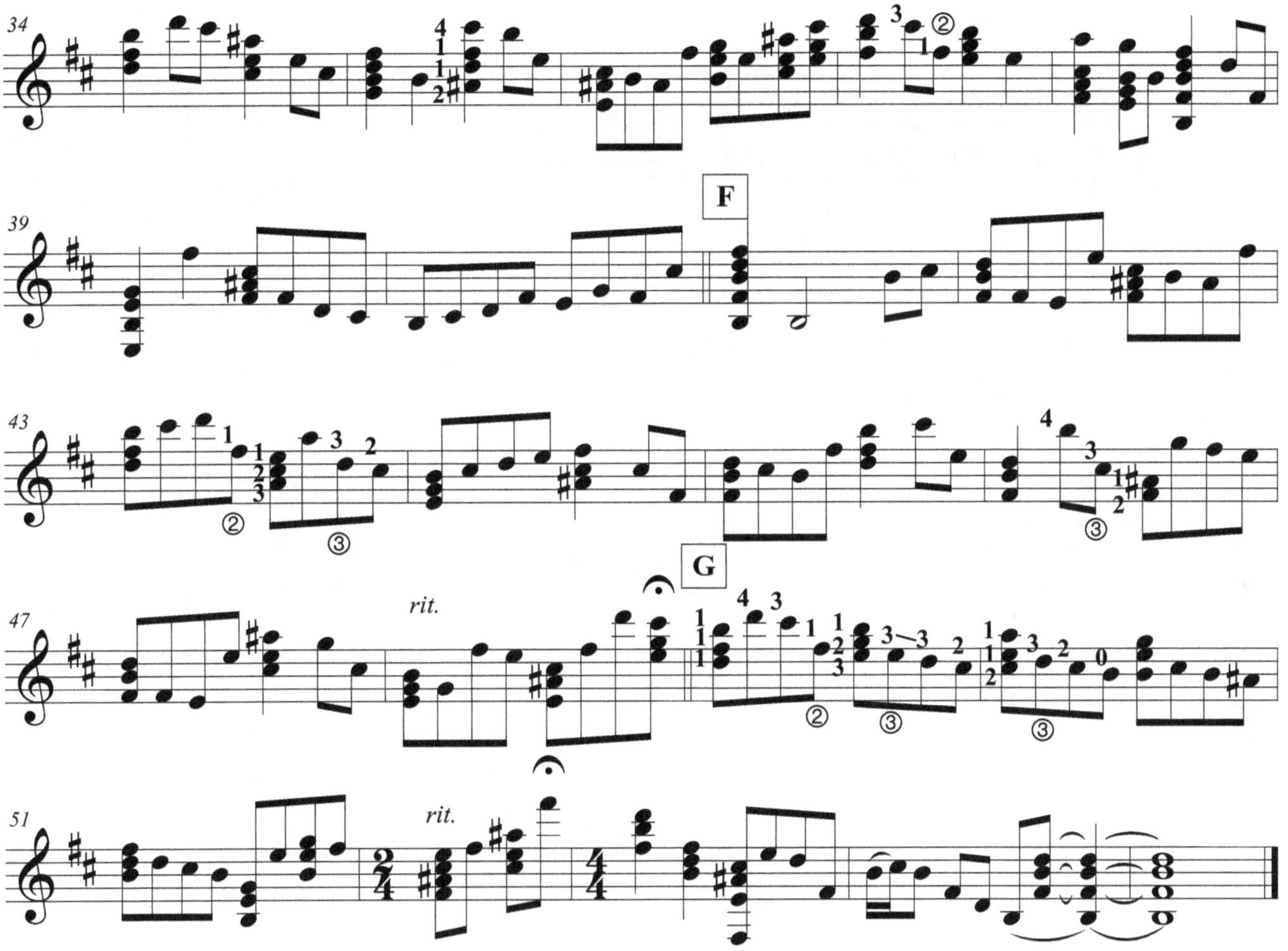
34
39
F
43
47
rit.
G
51
rit.

Prelude #8

William Bay

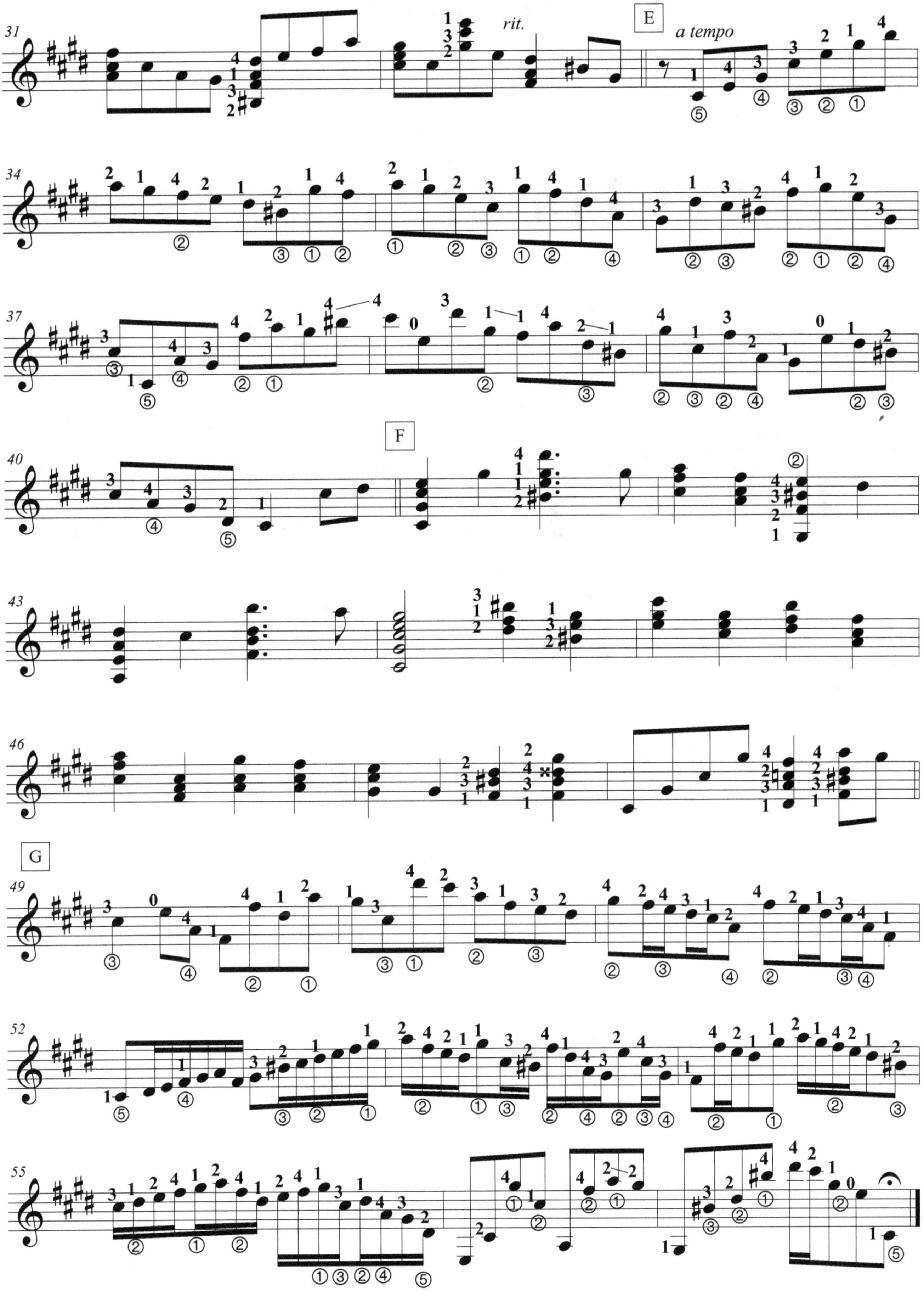
rit.
E
a tempo
F
G

Prelude #14

Dropped-D Tuning

Slowly ♩ = 100

William Bay

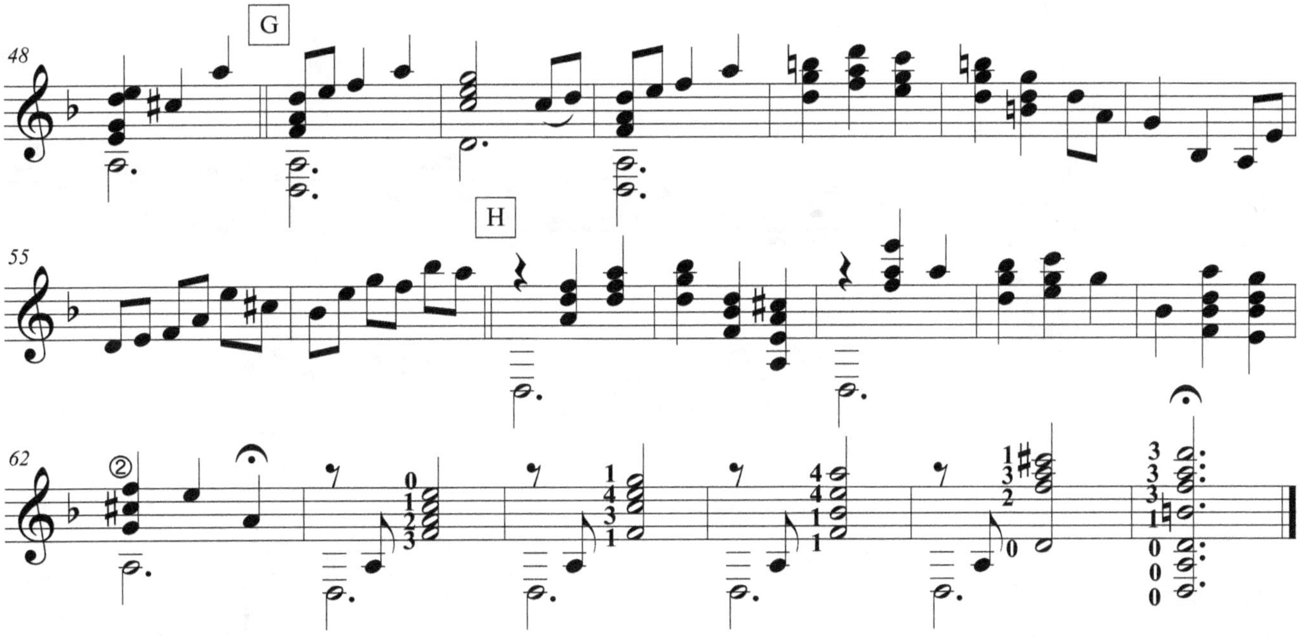
48
G
55
H
62

Horizon

William Bay

Slowly and Freely